YoungV

# Past Poets
# – Future Voices

## 2010 Poetry Competition for 11-18 year-olds

# The South & South West
# Of England

## Edited by Mark Richardson
## Helen Davies & Lisa Adlam

First published in Great Britain in 2010 by

 Young**Writers**

Remus House
Coltsfoot Drive
Peterborough
PE2 9JX
Telephone: 01733 890066
Website: www.youngwriters.co.uk

# Foreword

Young Writers was established in order to promote creativity and a love of reading and writing in children and young adults. We believe that by offering them a chance to see their own work in print, their confidence will grow and they will be encouraged to become the poets of tomorrow.

Our latest competition 'Past Poets - Future Voices' was specifically designed as a showcase for secondary school pupils, giving them a platform with which to express their ideas, aspirations and passions. In order to expand their skills, entrants were encouraged to use different forms, styles and techniques.

Selecting the poems for publication was a difficult yet rewarding task and we are proud to present the resulting anthology. We hope you agree that this collection is an excellent insight into the voices of the future.

# Contents

## Mangotsfield School, Bristol

## Nailsea School, Bristol

## Norbury Manor Business College, Thornton Heath

## The Axe Valley Community College, Axminster

## Torquay Girls' Grammar School, Torquay

## Treviglas Community College, Newquay

## Wadham School, Crewkerne

## Wallington High School for Girls, Wallington

## West Hill School, Leatherhead

## Wey Valley School, Dorset

# The Poems

## Why Will I Not Cry?

Why?
Why will I not cry?
There is water all around me, but not in my eye
Not even the baby will cry
You don't need to ask why
To know why the baby will not cry
But is that the same reason why
I will not cry?

I had to say goodbye
To my mama that did cry
That still does cry
And to all my family that did cry
And that still does cry
But I didn't cry
And I still don't cry
Maybe there's no reason to cry
Because not even the baby will cry

I had to say goodbye
To my country that did cry
That still does cry
And with its people that did cry
And that still do cry
But I didn't cry
Maybe there's no reason to cry
Because not even the baby will cry

I am starting to think that this trip was a lie
The promise of life was a lie
Because the baby still doesn't cry
Neither do I.

**Alexandre Duguay (16)**
**ACS Hillingdon International School, Uxbridge**

**1**

## My Sin

Eerie, dreary, I mourn with weary eyes,
Weary eyes that sweep the skies,
Evoking emotions of that very demise,
I hear the mocking tides slash in foe
As I unfold my darkest woe.
Eerie, dreary, below here she lies aglow.

She powers my joy, yet she subdues my affection,
I cannot look in her direction,
Nor form a connection.
As I wear her wasted face in my disguise,
A disgrace cornered in this filthy maze,
Eerie, dreary, I now bear her in my gaze.

An eruption of voices fills the distance,
Flowing through my scars with stout insistence.
The craving lust for existence evades my own resistance.
As I falter down the icy spiral, my demons speak in choral,
I cling unto the essence of life in this quarrel,
Eerie, dreary, she now takes my morale.

Awake, I rise up mid-air,
In despair, I claim to a prayer,
A prayer for salvation and revival to declare.
As I flow without meaning in the midnight's sun,
I can see my sins have made me none,
Eerie, dreary, the silence has begun.

**Morten Urdal (16)**
**ACS Hillingdon International School, Uxbridge**

## Thunder On The Mountaintop

*'. . . But it doesn't really matter with me now,*
*Because I've been to the mountaintop . . .*
*And I have looked over*
*And I have seen the Promised Land!'*

- From Martin Luther King's final speech

Close, close to the floor,
Next to a window into the world
That takes up the world, close to
the ground, and soon, and now
the sound. The sound. The sound of thunder in the mountains.
When you wake to the sound
from the mountaintop,
You wake to the sound of the end of the world,
Close, close to the ground,
Deep in the sky, deep in your hands,
Head on the floor,
Lake spilling prophecies flooding the door,
Thunder spilling from your hands,
Thunder flooding the Promised Land.
The mountaintop. The mountaintop.
And I have been. And I've looked over.
And I have not seen. But I have heard.

**Mariella Hudson (16)**
**ACS Hillingdon International School, Uxbridge**

3

# Home

He runs down the stairs
To fetch a shirt.
The steps creak and crack
Under his weight.

He reaches the bottom floor
And sees her.

She is doing nothing wrong,
The pots click and clack
As she washes them.

Music is in her ears,
Heaviness in her heart.

She can't hear him,
She has no way of knowing
He is there.

*Creak, crack, click, clack,
Crash!*

And the music is gone.

**Angela Lamb (16)**
**ACS Hillingdon International School, Uxbridge**

## Absence

You're going far away, like a bird lost from its nest,
I know your absence will hurt me, but I've really got to try my best,
How far away is far away?
A mile, an ocean, or a lifetime?
We all know promises are all too easy to say,
But will you and I keep them when you're absent and far away?
Will I reminisce about our lifetime memories?
Or will they fade away and become moments of recollection?
If we follow through and use our determination,
The reward will be huge for the time of our dedication.

**Isabella Olivia Rose (15)**
**ACS Hillingdon International School, Uxbridge**

4

## What's It Like In Care?

Every day she says if I don't
Buck up with my behaviour
And buck up with my ideas
I'm going in care
I'm on an ASBO
I nicked things in shops
I popped a tyre
I smashed windows
I play football on the old school site
I'll get arrested if I don't go to school
The contract is hard to keep
I have to tell my mum where I am going
If I miss three days, I get arrested
If I don't take my phone out
If I damage things
If I do loads of things, I get arrested
How did I get into this naughtiness?
Since my dad died, I've missed him
I am angry and it makes me do it
It's getting worse
What is it like in care?

**Joshe Parker (13)**
**Brook Green Centre for Learning, Plymouth**

## Just Because

Just because I don't play doesn't mean I'm lazy
Just because I like basketball doesn't mean I am a sporty nerd
Just because I like school doesn't mean I'm not cool
Just because I find things difficult doesn't mean I am a fool
Just because I can't hear properly doesn't mean I'm not listening
Just because I am lip reading doesn't mean I'm staring
I am deaf, so I'm different to everyone else
I am special and I'm at a special school
But I want people to treat me the same as everyone else.

**Lewis Taylor (13)**
**Brook Green Centre for Learning, Plymouth**

**5**

## Just Because

Just because I play on my Xbox 360
Doesn't mean I am dark.
Just because I like Bakugan
Doesn't mean I am a baby.
Just because I don't like school
Doesn't mean I don't learn hard.
Just because I don't like football
Doesn't mean I don't like sport.
Just because I like chocolate
Doesn't mean I don't eat fruit.
Just because I am funny
Doesn't mean I'm a clown.
I'm just me
Take me how I am.

**Rhys Harry (12)**
**Brook Green Centre for Learning, Plymouth**

## War

Bullets are flying
People are dying
Soldiers are diving
The sky's alarming
And
It is bright everywhere
The flares are bright and alarming
The shrapnel is alarming
My God, everybody is dying
Mothers and daughters
And sons and fathers
Are crying

What is this war all about?

**Sean Edwards (14)**
**Brook Green Centre for Learning, Plymouth**

6

## Bad Boys

Bad boys, bad boys,
We are coming for a fight.
So what are ya gonna do?
We're not afraid of you.
You'd best stand tall,
Because we are coming for a brawl.
We are round the corner,
You'd better come now,
Or if you don't,
I will get you like you got my friend,
That is a promise,
This war will end!

**Adam Stacey (14)**
**Brook Green Centre for Learning, Plymouth**

## The Never-Ending War

I was the last man standing as many people died
I picked up a different weapon and put on a mask
Then high in the sky, I heard a bag blast
I thought this day was going to be the last
Day I would live to tell this story to you
Then all of a sudden, the sun came out
And I heard people begin to shout
'You're not on your own
We are here to help you win this battle'
The days went by
And we won the war.

**Matthew Lewis (13)**
**Brook Green Centre for Learning, Plymouth**

# Soldier's Prayer

The day we were born,
The day we blew the horn.
We all cry,
But someday you will have to say goodbye.
The day we lay,
The day the farmers lay the hay,
The day the soldiers go on their way.
The day we put our hands together and start to pray,
That all the aggression will go away.

**Corey McGrath (13)**
**Brook Green Centre for Learning, Plymouth**

## The War In Afghanistan

Soldiers are firing at the enemy,
Some people are dying,
Someone is yelling,
Lives are lost,
Bombs are dropping,
Soldiers are fighting,
Scraping the enemy,
Soldiers are clashing,
I am the last soldier standing.

**Ashley Liversidge (14)**
**Brook Green Centre for Learning, Plymouth**

## Just Because

Just because I play with my dogs doesn't mean I have no friends
Just because I listen to loud music doesn't mean I have no feelings
Just because I play with my friends doesn't mean I leave out my family
Just because I'm not the same as you doesn't mean I don't like you
Just because you are not the same as me doesn't mean that you can't like me.

**Cara Ramsay (13)**
**Brook Green Centre for Learning, Plymouth**

## Mixed Emotions

Sad when I am getting bullied
Upset if I can't defend myself
Angry when I get bullied
Furious if they don't let me go
Worried when my friends get bullied
Scared if they go in my face
Supported when I call the police
Hopeful if I don't get bullied.

**Rhys McGlinchey (16)**
**Brook Green Centre for Learning, Plymouth**

## Brightly

Brightly the moon did shine high in the sky,
Brightly the moon began to cry,
Brightly the moon fell asleep,
Brightly now it was time to wake,
Brightly the sun smiled at his mate,
Brightly the sun got hot,
Brightly the moon went home,
Brightly the sun was left on his own.

**James Clifford (13)**
**Brook Green Centre for Learning, Plymouth**

## Snooker Loopy

Pot a ball all around
Then up and down
Off the red and kiss the brown
Pot all the colours to get 147
I love snooker
Snooker loopy am I!

**Corey Martin (12)**
**Brook Green Centre for Learning, Plymouth**

## Watch Out, Green Army

Watch out, watch out, green army fighter
Watch out, watch out, knives are coming round
Watch out, watch out, people getting stabbed
Watch out, watch out, lots of blood.

**Joshua Bishop (11)**
**Brook Green Centre for Learning, Plymouth**


## Just Because

Just because I'm cheeky doesn't mean I'm rude
Just because I like school doesn't mean I'm boring
Just because I like 'TV Burp', doesn't mean I like to burp
Just because I like robots, doesn't mean I come from another planet.

**Ethan Parker (12)**
**Brook Green Centre for Learning, Plymouth**


## Just Because

Just because I like 'Top Gear' doesn't make me a nerd
Just because I don't like sport doesn't make me a fool
Just because I like Homer Simpson doesn't mean I like doughnuts
Just because I am talkative doesn't make me a chatterbox.

**David Marks (12)**
**Brook Green Centre for Learning, Plymouth**

## Rain

It thunders down, violently drumming away,
It screams as it pours, it's set in for the day,
Endless waves sweep through the air,
Crashing to the ground,
The rain continues to gracefully throw itself around.

Falling faster, wailing winds, it's a terrible sight,
Crashing quicker, hammering harder, it give you quite a fright,
Rain pours, thunder claps and lightning crashes,
The great yellow sparks appear in sudden flashes.

But the great king dies out, like a flickering flame,
Finally, the monster is tame,
But the land is covered in crystal-clear water,
In the long, tiring day grown shorter.

**Brooke Hillier (13)**
**Chipping Sodbury School, Chipping Sodbury**


## Finding You

Finding you is like finding a light
In what seems to be a never-ending tunnel
That shows me the way back to safety and civilisation.

It's like being cured of blindness
And seeing my favourite sights again
Like the flowers bending in the breeze
Or the sunset in a clear summer sky.

Now I have found you
We can share a kiss
As my heart fills with eternal bliss
You make me smile on the inside and out.

**Stephanie Dando (13)**
**Chipping Sodbury School, Chipping Sodbury**

**11**

# Love And Hate

I love the way my mum laughs
I love to be in fashion
I love my dog's face
I love my trampoline
I love watching movies
I love the way my dog tries to talk to me
I love lots of handbags
I love most animals
I love my mum's hugs
I hate the way spiders crawl on you
I hate that my grandad has passed away
I hate eating things that I don't like
I hate to be embarrassed
I hate to be scared
I hate my dad's hair

But there's one thing that I love and hate
And that's life.

**Alicia Boore (12)**
**Denefield School, Reading**

## Autumn Creatures

When the trees are golden
And it's crisp outside
And the birds fly south
And in comes the tide,
To wash away the sculptures,
From summer holidays
And the hibernating creatures,
Prepare their hideaways,
Then out come the fairies
And pixies and elves
And they tidy our gardens,
All by themselves
And they rake all the leaves
And they shape the trees,
They brighten the sun
And blow the nice breeze
And they dance in a ring,
Round the mulberry bush
And they chase and they hide
And each other they push
And they tickle and they tease
And put flowers in their hair
And when crawling through thorns,
It's their clothes they tear,
But when winter comes,
It's homewards they fly,
They bid hedgehogs goodnight
And to us, say goodbye.

**Joanna Stell (12)**
**Hardenhuish School, Chippenham**

13

# The Sea

The sea,
Angry and blue;
A dog,
Swiping at the shore,
The rocks,
The cliffs,
Yowling and thrashing,
Screeching and screaming,
Willing to break over the border,
The border holding it back;
Squeezing and compressing it.

The sun sets,
The sea's fighting weakens,
He gives in,
Stretching out,
Yawning and calming,
He sleeps,
Silent,
Waiting again,
To be unleashed.

**Rosemary Webster (12)**
**Hardenhuish School, Chippenham**

## Mummy, I Love You

Mummy, please let me eat,
I'll eat anything,
Mouldy cabbage, rough meat,
Anything.

My belly is empty,
My clothes have holes and I wear only one shoe,
I'm scared I might starve,
What should I do?

Please, I love you,
Tell me, what did I do?
My stomach is so skinny,
You can see right through.

I haven't eaten for a week now,
So I feel like I'm going to die,
Why doesn't my mummy love me?
Why does she make me cry?

I sleep in the dog's bed,
My clothes are in bags,
My mummy says I'm too sissy to smoke
That's why I smoke fags.

My real name is Emily,
But my mummy calls me a bad name,
I really don't want to say it,
Because it really hurts my feelings and gives me lots of pain.

I'm a six-year-old girl
And my mummy beats me up,
She says she doesn't love me,
Whilst drinking from a cup.

**Amy Sharpe (12)**
**Harrow High School & Sports College, Harrow**

## Tables Will Turn

All alone, no one around
I'm falling to the ground
My world is full of pain, misery and pain
You look upon me with disdain
Always seeking your approval
All I get is refusal.

In darkness I live
Never positive
My mind is bleak
When I speak
Not one person listens
It's like my mouth is moving
But no sound is projecting.

Karma is lurking
Undercover it's working
It will push you to the brink
Soon will you sink
Now the doors will open up for me
So you can have my life of misery.

This is just the beginning
Like the shore of the sea
Coming at you like a dart
This is just the start!

**Ciara Murphy (13)**
**Harrow High School & Sports College, Harrow**

## There Was A Young Man From Dundee

There was a young man from Dundee
Who made up a Mii on the Wii
He wore a purple hat
And really looked quite fat
All dressed up like Nanny McPhee.

**Caleb Marchant (13)**
**Lakeside Secondary School, Eastleigh**

16

## Happiness

My mum is always there
In time of need and care,
Sometimes she is sad
Or sometimes she is mad,
But
I love her very dear
And she is always here,
She always gives me hope
To make me cope,
So
A message to my mum
The most loved one,
I know I can be a pain
But you always love me again.

Love from
Luke.

**Luke Harland (13)**
**Lakeside Secondary School, Eastleigh**


## Remember, Remember

Remember, remember
The fifth of November
When Guy Fawkes got caught.
He thought he was hard
To blow up the yard
And his plans all came to nought!

We think of him now
When we scream so loud
As the fireworks all go round.
So sorry he got caught
But he shouldn't have ought
Argued with who got crowned!

**Rhys Tindall & Luke Harland (13)**
**Lakeside Secondary School, Eastleigh**

**17**

# There Was A Young Man Called Brandon

There was a young man called Brandon
Who did not support teams at random
Man United was his
When they did the biz
Sounding like a plane that was landing.

**Brandon Heald (13)**
**Lakeside Secondary School, Eastleigh**

## War Poem

The night was as dark as a tunnel
And explosive as a boom
And as scary as if the world was ending . . .

It was as if there was nothing we could do.

**Sam George (15)**
**Lakeside Secondary School, Eastleigh**

## Clever Trevor

Clever Trevor, a hero, yes
Clever Trevor is the best
The team have won the cup again
Will next season be the same?

**Ashley Smith (13)**
**Lakeside Secondary School, Eastleigh**

## Summer

S un and smiles all around
U gly days go away
M elting ice lollies dripping everywhere
M ingling with friends at the fair
E verlasting days of fun
R oasting people in the sun.

**Emily Collins (13)**
**Liskeard School & Community College, Liskeard**

## Jump To Death

I stand there,
Shaking in the rain,
Taking punch after punch,
My body numb with pain.

The sound of demons chanting,
Ringing in my ears,
With every blow, I'm fighting,
Against the bitter tears.

That final blow,
That fist so hard,
The bruise may heal,
But I'm forever scarred.

I want to end it now,
I want to stop the pain,
I want to leave that fist that strikes
Again and again and again.

I want to abandon the world of hurt,
That stabs me every day,
But only now do I realise,
The price I have to pay.

I look down at the water,
That stares me in the face,
I can end the suffering now,
With just one single pace.

I take a step, I fall,
The water's there to meet me,
I plunge into the icy depths,
Death is there to claim me.

I'm in another world,
With another pain,
For though I have escaped,
I shall never live again.

**Lindsey Ruth Day (13)**
**Liskeard School & Community College, Liskeard**

**19**

# We Are Wonderful

We are as free as a butterfly,
As free as a bee,
Free as the waves lapping on the sea.

We are as strong as a brick,
As strong as a tree,
Strong as the dream waving a key.

We are as gentle as a cloud,
As gentle as a touch,
Gentle as wind thrashing with a rush.

We are as fast as a leopard,
As fast as a car,
Fast as a plane taking off afar.

We are as bright as the sun,
As bright as a book,
Bright as the torch shining a look.

We are as living as the dead,
As living on the world,
Living as the child I am.

We are as cool as an ice cream,
As cool as the sea,
Cool as the ice cubes in the cold tea.

We are as fun as a game,
As fun as being lame,
Fun as playing a card game.

We are as happy as a smiley face,
As happy as a waggy-tail dog,
Happy as a lazy, fat mog.

We are all these wonderful things,
As wonderful as the world,
Wonderful as this poem coming to an end!

**Nicole Harding (13)**
**Liskeard School & Community College, Liskeard**

## An Unlucky Event

A small, young boy,
So sweet and kind,
But never received much,
Not even a toy.

His pure, soft face,
His rosy cheeks, perfect,
But soon a death,
His life, taken in a race.

He was doing alright,
At the start, that is,
Until he grew faint,
All pale and white.

His small smile sunk,
He fell to the ground,
The people around him,
They began to surround.

His small heart shrunk,
His breathing stopped,
He was soon in a black box,
In a black car's trunk.

The asthma had got him,
He was no more,
He passed on the lights,
His expression, dim.

Tears were shed,
He lay there cold,
Everyone was dressed in black,
He lay there, dead.

Whispers and prayers shared,
Every tear that day, full of love.

**Emily Anne McKenna (13)**
**Liskeard School & Community College, Liskeard**

21

# Compassion

Where is the point in a little compassion?
It is a deed but heedless of a larger picture
An act but tactless in carefully crafting
Your miraged image (temporarily lasting)

Not as noted as a potent kindness
A little compassion is a misplaced, mindless
Attempt at soothing a smaller sadness, finding
The only benefit is a quiet gladness

Since the only apparent situation
Deserving of such, is compensation
In established friendships, requiring
An orthodox, healthy relation of minds
No finding, no learning, false elation
In this self-helping act of being kind

Yet the beaming, damp dog will lick from the fun
Of the day, to share joy 'neath the blinding bright sun
And the factory worker may be content for a while
That what they construct may perchance cause a smile
As the trundling youngster spies a snail on hard ground
That it picks up, places in parents' flowerbed and feels proud

I say throw thought to the cold, channelled wind of normality
And drift through the harrowed old walls of 'formality'
To see 'beneath' not in status but a fortuned position
While, earnest, instead, is earning volitions
To mildly echo that good Samaritan
May be, not past, but outside comparison

To sink past a haughty, unlasting exterior, to
Think lasting thoughts of the goodness of small
Acts of compassion between all equal souls
You may see that compassion is the point of it all.

**Zach Leon (18)**
**Liskeard School & Community College, Liskeard**

## The Royal English Breakfast

The royal white bread
With royal creamy butter
Royal strawberry jam
With crisp brown toast
The royal breakfast
Nothing like supper

The kings and queens
Princes and princesses
Gather for supper
But nothing can beat
English breakfast done properly.

Five o'clock, seven o'clock, eight o'clock,
Whatever time you take it
It's clear to me
When eating royal food
Breakfast is better

Whether you have cornflakes
Weetabix or even toast
Don't you see
It so beats tea
The royal breakfast is so much better

Now isn't it clear to you too
Now there's only one thing to do
I would write more
But I can't be bothered
Time for me to have royal English breakfast
Done
Proper!

**Emily Allis (12)**
**Liskeard School & Community College, Liskeard**

23

# My Poem About A Poem

I wrote a poem about a poem,
About a poem,
About a poem,
About a poem,
That goes like

I wrote a poem
And what a lovely poem it was
I wrote it whilst I was sewing
And I wrote it because

I know lots about poems
There are rhyming ones
There are ones that don't rhyme
There are small ones
And ones that take time

There are lots of poems people have written
They write them about the strangest things
There are some about family
There are some about being gobsmacked
There are some about the sea
There's even one about tarmac

Lots of people have written poems
Even if it takes them a lot of time
There are some about rowing
Now do you want to hear mine?

It goes like . . .

I wrote a poem about a poem
About a poem . . .

**Athalie Redgrove (13)**
**Liskeard School & Community College, Liskeard**

24

## Our Day Out

I sat there, looking around
On top of the cliff
Briggsy was staring
As I said I would jump

He told me not to
He told me why
I listened to him
As he smiled

He's never grinned
In his life
And that's the reason
I didn't jump

I took his hand
But suddenly
My foot slipped in the sand
He held me tightly

He was like a parent
Soft and gentle
He took me back to the bus
And didn't even go mental

Nothing else was said
When we went back to school
Mr Briggs was nice
And the school changed . . .

. . . Completely.

**Blake Penhaligan & Mark Arnold (12)**
**Liskeard School & Community College, Liskeard**

## Second Chance

Getting straight to the point
(As I always do)
I yelled and screamed at the young girl
She looked at me bright-eyed and scared
She looked at me blankly she didn't have a clue
She stared into space as if this was a dream

She glanced down the cliff
Hesitating for a second
She shifted uneasily, steadily, cautiously
Edging to the cliff

At that moment I guessed
At that moment I realised
She would and could jump
But why?
Why would she end her life here and now?
Why had she stopped hoping?

I changed my strategy
I changed my goal
My voice got lighter, friendlier, nicer
I changed her mind
I made her realise
That she could have a second chance
A brand new start.

**Millie Whitehead (13)**
**Liskeard School & Community College, Liskeard**


## Winter

W ind blowing
 I  gloos being built
N ights getting longer
T rees covered in snow
E ating soup to warm us up
R ain, rain, rain.

**Courtney Rollason (13)**
**Liskeard School & Community College, Liskeard**

## On The Edge

I stood on the edge
My body swaying in the wind
Leaning further
Towards the end

The world came alive
And I was part of it
For a moment
Just one

This I shall miss
The rain and wind
The thrill
Before the fall

My breath, my heartbeat
Gentle and small
So easy
To destroy

But for once
I have the power to take
My life
In my hands

Forever is now
Now is forever.

**Leah Merrifield (13)**
**Liskeard School & Community College, Liskeard**

## Disowned

I walked off
To me the world had already ended
Somehow
Sitting on that cliffside, swinging my legs
Life came into perspective.

Why?
Why should we be treated the way we are?
With people saying we should be locked up
Like animals
Just because we're different to them
Why?

I found myself flying
My life flashed in front of me
A shiver went down my spine
I wasn't scared
It was a feeling of relief.

The relief from the life I hadn't been living
The relief from the spiteful muttering
The nasty glares
The mistrust from everyone.

It would be over.

Things would be better.

**Charlotte Oatridge (13)**
**Liskeard School & Community College, Liskeard**

## Summer Fun

Summer is really fun
You get to see lots
Of the sun
It's here
It's there
It's everywhere
Summer is really fun.

You get to see your mates
And go on lots of dates
Go to parties, go to clubs
Go to discos, go to pubs
Go with your mums and your bruvs
Summer is really fun.

You go outside and sunbathe
Or stay inside and pray
That the sun will come in and give you a nice sun ray
Go to the beach, go in the sea
But watch out for those bumbling bees
And eat a nice ice cream
You do all this in summer
While eating bread and butter
All you need to remember, is
Summer is really fun!

**Kelsie Worth (13)**
**Liskeard School & Community College, Liskeard**

## Friends

F is for forever friendship
R is for remembering all of our good times
I is for no longer independent
E is for everlasting love
N is for never-ending close friends
D is for drama queens
S is for sympathy - what I get when I'm down.

**Becky Picariello (13)**
**Liskeard School & Community College, Liskeard**

**29**

## Summer

School is over
It's time to relax

There's lots to do
So you better prepare

Get the BBQ out
On this great summer's day

It's time to sleep
But it's still light outside

It's an early night
Until the next summer's day

The sun has risen, it's time to get up
It's a brand new day, it's a brand new life

Wake up, England, it's summer outside
It's time for the beach

The roads are packed, but it will be worth it
For a great summer's dip

Summer is dead and so are the trees
As their hair falls off

Now it's another year
To another great summer's day.

**Aaron Floyd (11)**
**Liskeard School & Community College, Liskeard**

30

## Paths . . .

Should I go there, should I stay here?
Should I be a bird flying high in the sky?
Could I love him, could I hate him?
Could I be a tree watching the days go by?

Did I make the right choice today?
Did I make myself look like a clown?
Did I make my friend feel happy?
Or did I make my friend feel down?

Should I have told that little white lie?
Am I the witch for doing that?
Maybe I should have told the truth
And been the dealer of the truce.

All the time I am in the middle
Of paths turning in all directions,
Some I take make me feel proud,
Others I take, I regret.

Every path opens a new door,
With rainbows and bunnies and hearts and flowers,
Any second the route can change,
But that is up to no one but me,
Life is an adventure on its own,
Filled with memories you'll never forget.

**Alice Gundry (13)**
**Liskeard School & Community College, Liskeard**

# Understanding

I saw her face
And understood
I felt empty
And thought

*What is she feeling?*
*Sadness? Hope?*
She was feeling free
For once

She had escaped home
And forgotten life
She felt normal
And hopeful

She was scared
And worried
And all shaky
I could see the fear in her eyes

She leapt!

My whole body tensed
And for that second
I knew her
And she knew me.

**Ellen Taylor (13)**
**Liskeard School & Community College, Liskeard**

# No Scope Kills

N uke
O ne man army

S entry gun
C all of Duty
O mnicide
P recision air strike
E levators.

**Nathan Tucker (12)**
**Liskeard School & Community College, Liskeard**

32

## My Dad

The boat bobs on the water top,
The tanned sailor sits,
Thinking, thinking of his family far,
He feels lonely, left out,
He feels no one loves him.

Then he remembers why he is there,
Not to think of his family far,
But of his duty to the world,
He knows people love him,
That's why he is there.

Sorrow fills his heart,
He is lonely, afraid,
The sea around him roars to frighten,
It spits and shouts,
The sailor is anxious.

His time is up,
The boat slows down,
People are cheering, screaming and shouting,
Everyone is happy to see him,
He is home.

He is my dad.

**Jenny Wood (12)**
**Liskeard School & Community College, Liskeard**


## ?

Guess what this is, it's not a quiz
It's more of a test, as you would have guessed
It's sometimes orange, but mostly green
But you've probably already seen
It has wings, it also sings
It has a face made of a shoelace
It's on the wall, it's very tall
It's my pet brick, so leg it, quick!

**Ashleigh Pay (13)**
**Liskeard School & Community College, Liskeard**

**33**

# Carol On The Cliff

The ocean lapped on the beach below
And the waves crashed on the rocks.
It seemed so quiet,
I could hear the birds calling in the fresh afternoon sky,
I thought of home.

The feeling of shock shot up my spine
And fear took over my body.
It left me trembling and filled with doubt
What would happen?
What would happen if I jumped?

I stood up shakily,
I took the leap.

My life stopped for a fragment of a second,
But in that second, I felt free, careless,
As if nothing in the world mattered.
Falling through the air like an innocent child in this cruel world,
In this moment, I had found who I was.

And then silence.

What could I feel?

Nothing.

**Rachael Jones (13)**
**Liskeard School & Community College, Liskeard**


# Michael Jackson

MJ isn't really dead
He lives in Brazil in a shed
He teaches orphans how to dance
To Lady GaGa's 'Bad Romance'
He likes to play football with Ghandi
And enjoys eating lots of candy
He farms cut-price bananas
In his Spider-Man pyjamas.

**Ethan Fursman (13)**
**Liskeard School & Community College, Liskeard**

## The Magic Box
*(Inspired by 'Magic Box' by Kit Wright)*

In my box . . .
There is a bag of bacon flavoured crisps
And a mat the size of a swimming pool.

In my box . . .
My strict gymnastics teacher is ready for my next lesson,
Holding my bottle for break.

In my box . . .
A dragon roars with a soft voice,
His fire made of salt, body made of pepper.

In my box . . .
A horse with no tail, canters around,
Looking for a mate.

In my box,
A blizzard whirls,
In the ragged mountains.

My box is fashioned
With sapphires and rubies,
Its hinges are the knuckles of a dinosaur,
In the corners, the voices of my loving family whisper jokes.

**Rachel Woodley (12)**
**Liskeard School & Community College, Liskeard**

## The Wonderful Life Ahead!

Bring your life by waking up
Having fun and living your life
Seeing your friend and no one to stop you
Your life is a wonderful and great place
Everyone has one, so should you
So go and live your life
And don't forget to have so much fun
Live your life like everyone lives theirs.

**Kennedy Waters (13)**
**Liskeard School & Community College, Liskeard**

## Freedom

It's our day out
Get away from school
Everybody shout
This will be cool.

Kids being bad
Or being good
'Stop it, lad,'
Said Briggs, where he stood.

Mister Briggs taking charge
Telling everybody off
Even when they barge
Or have a cough.

They go to the zoo
With all the animals
Each taking two
Briggs shouts at them all.

The zoo is empty
The keeper finds out
The children have plenty
So the keeper must shout.

**Zach Davies (12)**
**Liskeard School & Community College, Liskeard**


## Tarmac

Tarmac is black, tarmac is cool,
Tarmac is what we have at school.
Tarmac gets hot in the sun
And burns your bum.
It's hard and if hit
Turns into shards.
So let's sing for tarmac, a wonderful thing,
Before they make some better bling.

**Samuel Hooper (11)**
**Liskeard School & Community College, Liskeard**

## He Is Never Gone

Really, what had I done wrong?
The news of his death in a whisper
No one really talked about it
Until I heard him say, 'I miss her'

A car misdirected, my husband resurrected
That is what it does seem
But when I heard him in my ear
Alive is he in my dreams

In my dreams I see him
In my dreams he sings to me
In my dreams he reaches out to touch my hand
In my dreams, it's no fantasy

But really, he is here right now
My heart is touched by his song
I feel his presence, I feel his peace
With me he comes along.

I honestly thought I'd lost him
But really, I'd just found
He may be in my dreams
But he'll always be around.

**Stephanie Greatorex (13)**
**Liskeard School & Community College, Liskeard**

## Moorland

M oors are green and brown
O ften covered in moss
O ver and over the wind will blow
R ain and thunder will wash the rocks
L ovely landscape all around
A lways a bird or two on a mound
N ever is it quiet
D eep ponds everywhere.

**Theo Tamblyn (13)**
**Liskeard School & Community College, Liskeard**

# Childhood Dreams

The interests of a minor
Around the age of five
Simplistic dreams with kings and queen
And castles stories high

My sister always told me
That it's just a fantasy
Real life is far more complicated
Than to a five-year-old it may seem

Hatred spills from poisoned lips
Heaven moves further away
Fists and guns and language foul
That nobody should say

The thing about my sister
Is she always tends to lie
Blaming her problems on others
Feeling sorry, she tends to cry

So I don't believe that rubbish
Because I know it's all wrong
My beliefs and imagination
Are far, far too strong.

**Joanna Peters (12)**
**Liskeard School & Community College, Liskeard**

## The Moonlit Moor

The moonlit moor,
Lay in silence,
Thinking of what's beyond the hills.

Across the moor,
The trees spied,
As they listened carefully.

In a nearby stream,
Fish dance in the moonlit water.

Another mine collapses,
Uncovering hidden treasure.

Trees crash,
Birds zoom by.

Bushes rustle,
Stars undress before bed.

The moonlit moor,
Lay in silence,
Waving goodbye.

**Kaja Vineer (12)**
**Liskeard School & Community College, Liskeard**


## Anger

I get angry
I go red
I feel sad
I hurt myself
I hurt everyone around me.

I love
My mum
My brothers
My sisters.

I don't mean to hurt them.

**Zac Cooper (13)**
**Liskeard School & Community College, Liskeard**

**39**

## Glimmer In The Corner

There it is
The glimmer in the corner
A whisper of glow in the dark
The weird sensation
The tickle within it
The glow that ignites in your heart.

The whisper of thread
In that special little corner
In the mind of the woman
Or the man who told her.

It sways in the corner
With a sparkle of light
In the dark of the corner
Or the broad daylight.

The compassion in the air
And the soft, warm feeling
The delicate love
And words are full of meaning.

**Beth Allen (12)**
**Liskeard School & Community College, Liskeard**


## Thanks To The Inventors Of Summer!

S unshine that shines in the summer
U p in the sky the sun shines bright
M olly, who we play with, lying in the sun
M ax we also play with, well, it is glorious weather
E ating an ice cream to cool you down
R ain during the night to cool the people asleep down

Our summer is cool
We like to go in the pool
Altogether we love our summer
And we are proud to have them around
Thanks to the inventors of summer!

**Kayleigh Scott (13)**
**Liskeard School & Community College, Liskeard**

## Poor Little Woodlouse And The Mean, Selfish Python!

Once, there was a little woodlouse
That lived in a little straw house
Then one day a camel came
And crushed the house and was in shame

The camel said, 'Sorry little woodlouse
I did not mean to crush your house
I'll build you a bigger woodlouse house!'

Once, there was a little woodlouse
That lived in a bigger, wooden house
Then one day a python passed
And crushed the house very fast

The python said, 'Sorry little woodlouse
I did not mean to crush your house
I'll get to it soon and build another!'

But the python never came
To build the woodlouse's house
So poor little woodlouse had no house!

**Elliot Grange (12)**
**Liskeard School & Community College, Liskeard**


## The Gift Of Life

I feel shaky and scared,
I feel closer to death,
I can't imagine dying,
My life is coming to an end,
I can feel it in my ice-cold blood,
I feel sick,
People are dying around me,
People I know and people I don't,
My life is over,
It makes me respect the gift of life,
They say life is cruel,
But really, it's the greatest gift of all.

**Joe May (13)**
**Liskeard School & Community College, Liskeard**

**41**

# The Wave

It builds up like tension
It falls like the rain,
Some can be strong
But they're mainly the same.

The sploshing, the splashing
The sound of the crash,
It's all calm right now
But here comes the splash.

The life down below are startled and scared
It was all so dramatic, you could tell that they cared,
It fell in a flash, like a fish with its fins
Sand, rocks and rubble swirled like the wind.

It all settled down, peace had returned
The weather and wind had suddenly turned,
Conditions outside were a lot more formal
Life had returned, it was finally normal.

**Marisa Coley (12)**
**Liskeard School & Community College, Liskeard**


# Rugby Hero

It's the last minute that could win us the league,
I have the ball in my hand,
Which is like having a piece of Heaven,
I run and run, more determined than ever,
But it was like I got struck by lightning,
As one of the opposition tackled me,
As I dropped to the ground,
There was a silence, but I got up,
Going this way, that way,
Tricking them more than ever
And scoring the winning try,
The ref blew the final whistle,
I was a rugby hero.

**Kimberley Bickle (13)**
**Liskeard School & Community College, Liskeard**

**42**

## The Reflection Of The Mirror

Standing there, looking into the reflector
Wondering if there is anything out there to protect her
The background behind me is all dull and dark
And then when I remember her smile, there comes that bright spark.

Anger and stress seems to take over
For all of my feelings seem to grow lower and lower
Calming down, I see slowly my mood changes
Tears rolling down my face, as it rearranges.

I turn my back on my eventful mirror
Just seeing the flashback when I saw the killer
For when I turn back around, I no longer see the darkness
I see my face smiling with all my happiness.

The oppression is gone
And I open the door
Feeling safe and loved
And cared for once more!

**Sophie Holder (12)**
**Liskeard School & Community College, Liskeard**

# Hair

Hair can be long,
Hair can be frizzy
Or wavy!
Hair can be short
Or maybe even
Straight!
Hair can be pink
Hair can be blue
Up or down . . .
You decide!
Hair can be any shape
Or style
You like!

**Emma Smith (12)**
**Liskeard School & Community College, Liskeard**

**43**

# The Beach

The golden sand;
Getting a tan;
The slippery rocks,
Even some docks.

The boats come in;
The lighthouse's dimmed,
The swishing sea,
The windy breeze;
Cools you down on a hot summer's day.

Going swimming;
Seeing the fish,
A jellyfish squished,
The coral rocks,
Like colourful clocks.

Buying fish and chips and ice cream
Just like a summer dream.

**Ellie Brodey (12)**
**Liskeard School & Community College, Liskeard**


# I Am . . .

No one knows who I am
No one knows where I am
No one knows what I am
All they know is that I am here

Some say I am an alien
Some say I am a beast
Some say I am a freak
All they say is I am here

Some write I am in Asia
Some write I am at the North Pole
Some write I am in Europe
All they write is I am here.

**Charlie Badham (12)**
**Liskeard School & Community College, Liskeard**

## Sweeney Todd

'We all deserve to die,'
He sang, holding a barber's knife at his thigh . . .
Blood dripping on the floor
How many more?
Blood dripping on the floor
How many more?

Mrs Lovett's pies were famous
Whilst they were getting eaten
The customer doesn't know
It is the shop owner
He is supposed to be meeting . . .

Sweeney Todd
The Barber of Fleet Street
The guy you don't want to meet
A close shave indeed
*Bam!* You're pie meat . . .

**Laura Fergus (12)**
**Liskeard School & Community College, Liskeard**


## Grandad

I never got to say goodbye, or even say, 'I love you'
So now here's my chance to say a massive great big, 'Thank you'
Thanks for all the times we shared
I know you really cared
Thanks for all the happy times and the sad ones too
I know it didn't seem like it, but I was close to you
I wake up some mornings and think you are here
Then I start to realise and I feel a sudden fear
You taught me right from wrong
You taught me to be strong
I know I shouldn't cry
But I did watch you die
I know that my heart has sunk, but I'm really, really mad
Because you were a part of me, so thank you, my grandad.

**Devon Woods (13)**
**Liskeard School & Community College, Liskeard**

**45**

## The Black Plague

The streets were filled with rats and mice,
The hay-thatched cottages were desolate and painted with a blood-
red cross,
The cries of children could be heard from miles,
While slaughtered cats and dogs hung from washing lines,
They call it the Black Plague!

Ashes of criminals and non-Christians were scattered on the path,
Some houses were filled with poses and roses,
While others were stenched in poo,
Windows were smashed and doors were ruptured,
They call it the Black Plague!

Dead bodies piled a hideous mountain,
The sewers flooded with tears,
They call it the Black Plague!
The world looked upon a life of prosperity,
But all they got was death and destruction!

**Patrick Hall (12)**
**Liskeard School & Community College, Liskeard**


## The Thickest Chavs

They think they're so cool,
Because they don't go to school,
Their trackies down to their knees,
Yes! They walk like chimpanzees.
Funny hats the wrong way round,
Is it me or do they seem like a clown!
They drink, they smoke,
This ain't no joke!
They seem pretty thick,
All they do is take the mick,
'Innit,' is what they say
It makes them sound so gay,
Tough and hard is what it takes
The thickest chav is what it makes.

**Olivia Tandy (12)**
**Liskeard School & Community College, Liskeard**

## Slipping

The salty breeze was velvet,
The crashing waves were inside me,
There was only water and wind . . .

I felt the stiff fear encasing me,
The black barrier blocking my sight,
I imagined the coolness,
Which would soon melt my cage . . .

I snapped the barrier,
Chucked all my thoughts into the waves
And let my feet slip silently . . .

My body chased my feet,
As I twisted through thought,
Tumbling endlessly,
Into painless black . . .

**Caitlin Bucher-Flynn (13)**
**Liskeard School & Community College, Liskeard**

## Poverty Poem

Some people live in poverty
Some people live in wealth
Some people live with cholera
Some people live in health
Some people live differently to you
So why treat them differently than you would like them to treat you?
Some people work for 24 hours a day
Sometimes faint and lay there and lay
If you give, say a pound a week
You could give them the food they seek
A new property and say goodbye to poverty
They are people just like us
But still we look at them in disgust
They have feelings too
Treat them with respect and they will do the same too.

**Maddelaine Vallance (12)**
**Liskeard School & Community College, Liskeard**

# The World

Our world is dying
Our trees are wilting
All year long the sun is burning
The seas are rising
Our land is flooded
The air is polluted
The animals are gone
The Earth will die if no one helps it
Our humanity is fading
We are not who we were
We are animals
Killing the world we live on
All our work would have been for nothing
All our creatures, religions gone
In the blink of an eye.

**Jack Rudd (13)**
**Liskeard School & Community College, Liskeard**

# My Friend, Deanna

M ates
Y arn on forever

F orever friends
R unning around crazily
I diots in the making
E ndless fun
N ight parties
D ay and night without a fight

D isco dancing
E ating sundaes all day
A nswering all the questions in a magazine
N aughty
N utty dancing
A ll done in a day!

**Morwenna Hatherley (12)**
**Liskeard School & Community College, Liskeard**

## A Normal Day

They're fine when they're on their own,
But it's different when they're around others.

Their personalities change,
Just like they're from a different book.

They try to impress their friends,
By putting others down.

Not knowing where to go or what to say,
I just try to keep a distance.

If they as much as glance over,
I feel scared and intimidated.

Hopefully one day this life will end,
Just like this poem.

**Alex Maclean (12)**
**Liskeard School & Community College, Liskeard**


## The Poem Of Love

Love is like a second part of me,
It gives me sweet harmony.
It sang to me and I never hurled,
To me it's like another world.

Love can make you do funny things,
However, it makes me sing.
Love helps in many ways,
It makes my troubles go away.

Good wants this world to be full of love,
It helps everyone to rise above.
I love this world and it loves me and you,
So let's get together, just me and you.

**Ashley James Buchan (13)**
**Liskeard School & Community College, Liskeard**

**49**

# Life

Life is a complicated thing,
Problems all around,
Death, lies, fear and pain.

Life is a complicated thing,
Opportunities all around,
Love, kindness, friendship and a future.

Life is a complicated thing,
Highs and lows,
Emotions running wild,
Fears being realised,
Hearts being broken,
Life being lived.

**Zoe Croft (13)**
**Liskeard School & Community College, Liskeard**

# I Miss You

I wish I could see you every day
Because of the things I have to say.
When I have tears in my eyes
Because I miss you.
You stop me from crying
And give me a tissue.

You're simply amazing
And I have trust in you
Because you're my friend
And I love you
So the two words to say
Are thank you.

**Kirsty Jefford (12)**
**Liskeard School & Community College, Liskeard**

## The Eye Of The Tiger

The moon shines bright in the dark and eerie night
He moves and hides in the bushes below
His fur shines bright with a scary glow
His claws are sharp like a lumberjack's axe
His growl is fierce, like the mouth of the Devil
He strikes in silence, carrying his victim in his jaws of Hell
Tearing his prey from flesh to bone
That was the only thing the beast had known
Searching for his brothers and sisters
Killing all the misses and misters
Little kids run to bed
Because the eye of the tiger is upon your head.

**Reece Moxham (13)**
**Liskeard School & Community College, Liskeard**


## My Dog

My dog is so cute, so fluffy and petite,
All she likes to do is eat, eat, eat!

She is so lazy and sleeps all day,
But she always hugs me after a hard school day.

She lays on my bed and snuggles up with me,
She's crazy about me, can't you see!

She's so dopey and she'll do anything,
She bounds around the room, like a big, bouncy spring.

She is my dog, I love her so,
I will never let her go!

**Ezme Wells (12)**
**Liskeard School & Community College, Liskeard**

## Relief

It was four in the morning
When our house phone started to ring
I was scared, worried and anxious
Soon to be hushed.

I went to my nan's
Where we sat awake all night.

Twelve hours later
I went to see her
She was beautiful
My body shook with relief.

**Bethany Pollard (11)**
**Liskeard School & Community College, Liskeard**


## What Rhymes With Purple?

What rhymes with purple?
Nothing.
Blue rhymes with loo,
Pink rhymes with sink,
Poor, lonely purple,
Nothing to rhyme with.
Red rhymes with bed,
Green rhymes with machine,
Solitary purple, but maybe if we make up a word,
Like . . . slurple!

**Erin Duffy (12)**
**Liskeard School & Community College, Liskeard**

## The Sea

It curls around each other,
The surfer paints a line
And the coral fingers point to the sky.

It sparkles all day long,
The surfer crashes with a bang!
With a start, the seagulls fly up high.

This is the beach and the sea,
With all its ocean wonders,
You will never want to say goodbye!

**Tamar Davis (12)**
**Liskeard School & Community College, Liskeard**


## Call Of Duty

There is a game called COD,
The noobs with a brand new Mod,
I have 'World at War' on my iPod,

This game is the opposite of c\*\*p,
Especially with the new maps,
But it's a shame they haven't got double tap,

I hate all the noobs,
Running around with tubes
And when I get killed, it ruins my mood.

**Jake Brown (13)**
**Liskeard School & Community College, Liskeard**

## Inside Me

Just because I'm a teen
You call me naughty, you call me bad,
Other kids think it's totally rad!

It's because something is fizzing
And popping inside me,
It helps me be me!

I may be a little angry,
Perhaps a little sad,
But when it's all over,
We'll all be glad!

It's because something is bubbling
And wiggling inside me,
It helps me be me!

I'm going through a change,
Transforming, becoming a grown lad
And one day it'll help me become a dad!

So, don't shout at me,
Don't tease me,
Don't hurt me,
Because this change helps me be me!

**Louis Parsons (12)**
**Mangotsfield School, Bristol**

## Always Will Be Me

I'm real to me, but I can change
I'm unique, yet similar
I'm outgoing, but shy
In my life as me

I am young, but I feel older
I'm silly and smart
I like depressing rock music
And I'm a tomboy who likes nail polish

Others say I'm odd or weird
And I can disagree
Because I usually feel about them
The way they feel about me

I'm contradictive and confusing
Serious and goofy
Usually looking like an idiot
But at the same time, knowing right from wrong

I'm a teenager
And much, much more
Undoubtedly and willingly
I will and always will, be me.

**Rachel Di Nucci (14)**
**Mangotsfield School, Bristol**

55

## Under My Bed

Every night I hear it,
*Tap, tap, tap, tap,*
I've never, ever seen it,
All I can hear as I
Sit in my bed, is
*Tap, tap, tap, tap!*

Each night it's the same,
*Tap, tap, tap, tap,*
It's so scary,
I get really wary
And I hate the way it goes ...
*Tap, tap, tap, tap!*

By morning it stops,
But as my feet,
Swing out of bed,
The ghost from beneath,
Grabs them instead!

**Eve Shelton-Richards (12)**
**Mangotsfield School, Bristol**

## They Say . . .

If you looked at me, this is what you would see,
Just an average girl.
Though, through the eyes of those that despise,
I'm just a terrorising youth.
They say we're the baddies, not the good,
They say they would dispose of us if they could,
They say we're naughty, cruel and bad,
They say they were better when they were a lad,
They say we're a disgrace to us all,
They say they are our leaders, standing tall,
I say, stop!
We are the future of this generation,
We are the ones to shape the nation,
We are one.

**Becca Purrington (12)**
**Mangotsfield School, Bristol**

## Bad Day

I woke up in the morning and now I want it to end
I sat down on my desk in first lesson
And my table turned into a monster
And squished me into the wall
My ruler came out of my pencil case
Trying to cut my neck like a knife
As I was on my way to second lesson
My angry book fell out of my bag
Trying to trip me up
My chair keeps on going backwards and forwards
Like a scary roller coaster ride
And it's hard for me to write!

Can my day get any worse?
Help me, now!

**Acaica Hewings King (13)**
**Nailsea School, Bristol**

## A Bad Day

I'm having such a bad day
It started when I got into the shower
And the water decided to scald me
The list continues
Taps wanted to splash me in the face
The fridge over-freezes all my food
Rug trips me up
Pen gets angry at what I'm writing
So it pokes me in the eye
And finally, the paper gives me a paper cut
I've had such a bad day!

**Michela Lopresti (12)**
**Nailsea School, Bristol**


## A Bad Day

Today is my bad day
I sit on the chair
The chair jumps in my arms, hurts me!
I watch TV, the TV is really busy, it's angry!
I go to school, I use a pen, the pen runs away
Today is my bad day!
The computer punches me!
The chair kicks me!
The book runs away!
Oh, my goodness!
Today is my bad day!

**Ting Yue Dong (12)**
**Nailsea School, Bristol**

## My Pygmy Marmosets

This is a tale of the dwarf monkey
He is part of the primate family
Pygmy marmosets eat the sap out of trees
But they aren't an endangered species
Pygmy marmosets live in Brazil and Peru
But mothers give birth to not one, but two
They are so small, that they fit on my finger
I built them a tower out of pieces of Jenga
It likes to cuddle my big teddy bear
But I do look after it with a load of care.

**James Ham (13)**
**Nailsea School, Bristol**

## The Old Man

There was an old man who had a bad day
He took the bus but it went the wrong way
When he got back it was even worse
He had lost his wallet and had to take a purse!
The kettle avenged him, the cooking was bad
When the cupboard saw this, he was sad
The curtains ignored him, the TV looked dead
The old man slipped and hit his head
When he woke up, he was glad to be alive
Then he realised the TV had died!

**Chris Corlett (12)**
**Nailsea School, Bristol**

## A Bad Day At School . . .

My alarm clock forgot to wake me up
Because it was still sleeping!
My pen and paper poked and prodded my hands!
My shoes sniggered and tied my shoelaces together
And tripped me up!
I tried to sit down, but my chair ran away from the desk!
My tie had an evil look in its eye
And tried to strangle me!
So today has been a bad day
Who knows what will happen tomorrow!

**Marley Nelson (13)**
**Nailsea School, Bristol**

## Our Society

We were freed, but we're still in chains,
They fought so we could hate, rebel, revolt,
They marched and so we stood,

Media has portrayed the worst,
Seething at the seams,
Enough to make our forefathers,
Regret, repent, remorse.

We subsist in a society,
Full of shame,
Disgrace and discrimination,
By our peers.

Was it all worth it?
The struggle, conflict, hatred?
Yet there is a glimmer of hope,
Somewhere.

We were freed, but we're still in chains,
They fought so we could hate, rebel, revolt,
They marched and so we walk,
We walk so our children can run.

**Leanne Deans (13)**
**Norbury Manor Business College, Thornton Heath**

 60

## Teenage Stereotype

The tragic teenage stereotype,
In our minds is kinda dull,
I mean, the way we party
And act all smarty,
To the policemen on patrol,

Compares nothing to the slang talking,
Gun-wheeling rumours of today,
We wear hoodies now
And say, 'Kapow!'
To the idiots in our way,

We normally wear big hoop earrings
And our hair strung back tight,
With shoplifted goods
And heads under hoods,
We're the creatures of the night,

Striped sunglasses are our thing
And we drink alcohol daily,
Do the paper round,
Each Sunday sound,
But steal tips from little old ladies,

But . . . if you actually got to know us,
You'd see we aren't that bad,
The clothes are true
And the partying too
And maybe some are chavs,

But the guns and knives and alcohol,
Are restricted to those unlucky,
We're not all nuns,
But we'll get out our guns,
And you better hope you ducky.

**Phoebe Bower (14)**
**Norbury Manor Business College, Thornton Heath**

# The Chocolate Cake

The delicious chocolate cake that you put in the fridge
I opened the fridge and saw heavenly, dreamy, divine,
Adorable chocolate cake,
The attracting, luscious icing kept staring at me.

I am very sorry for what I did,
But your rich, lush chocolate cake,
Was so beautiful and delicious, that despite what I have said,
The cake tasted even better.

I was so tempted to eat it,
Because of the attracting, luscious icing and on the top of all
Of the tasty chocolate, there was a cherry as red as a rose,
Now this just told me to eat your chocolate cake.

I am very sorry for what I have done to your . . .

Rich,
Lush,
Delicious,
Heavenly,
Dreamy,
Divine,
Adorable,
Attracting,
Luscious,
Tasty
Chocolate
Cake.

By the way, please text or call me,
When you buy another

Rich,
Lush,
Delicious,
Heavenly,
Dreamy,
Divine,
Adorable,
Attracting,
Luscious,
Tasty
Chocolate cake.

**Jasleen Kaur Sandhu (11)**
**Norbury Manor Business College, Thornton Heath**

## Did You Ever Wonder . . . ?

Did you ever wonder,
About what it would be like,
If you could sometimes escape from it all,
To another place, another world, another dimension, another
universe?
Did you ever wonder?

In this world you would get what you wanted,
In this world you would feel in control,
In this world you would have success in every dream,
In this world you would fly like the wind,
Did you ever wonder?

Over here the streets would be made of solid gold,
Over there the street lamps would be made of crystals,
Over here the flowers would bloom into all shapes and colours,
Did you ever wonder?

This place will never be without any faith,
So close your eyes and always believe if not today, maybe tomorrow,
But remember you will always get there one day,
So, until then, you just have to wonder!
Did you ever wonder?

**Annum Abbas (12)**
**Norbury Manor Business College, Thornton Heath**

63

# My Past, My Present And My Future

I saw a mixture of emotions
As I gazed into my past,
I saw my family struggling and striving
Shadows on their present were cast.

I saw the happy times we had
My first birthday in the park,
My first word and my first step
Happiness that shed light upon the dark.

I saw all the bereavements we had
And with a melancholy sigh,
I saw the deaths, the pain, the tears
And I waved my past goodbye.

And as I come to my present
I see my hidden secrets,
The lies I've told, the things I've kept
The points where hope was weakest.

I see my family now and then
Compare them to my past,
The joys and expectations we share
Thank goodness we're here at last!

Now I see my friends, my school, ambitions
And I see exams coming by
And with a heavy sigh of relief
I wave my present goodbye.

Now I catch up with my future
Thinking it will be the best,
It will be the brightest time
It will outshine the rest.

Fortunately, I see myself as a heart surgeon
The profession of my dreams,
I've fulfilled my education
The goal of my life, it seems.

But as I look at the environment
Outside the border of dreams,
The air is filled with pollution

And the Earth itself does weep.

I think to myself, *where is our Earth*
*That we cared for so much before?*
*The Earth we took care of*
*And did everything we could do for?*

And then again, I think to myself
*Come, let's jump back in time,*
*To my present where we can change this*
*And brighten our future in time!*

**Rimel Naqvi (13)**
**Norbury Manor Business College, Thornton Heath**

## Where On Earth Am I?

I'm far away from my world,
I can't find a way back home,
I'm in need of some help,
Where on Earth am I?

I walk a little north,
I walk a little south,
I'll walk until I find a way
Where on Earth am I?

Strange creatures, big and small,
Some are short and some are tall,
I'll find one to help me home,
Where on Earth am I?

I'm getting scared,
I need some help, through this terrible scare,
I have to get home, I need to rest, I just can't bear it,
Where on Earth am I?

The night has gone and I wake up
It was all just a dream,
Until I go to sleep again,
I will know where on Earth I am!

**Rebecca Winkler (14)**
**Norbury Manor Business College, Thornton Heath**

**65**

## Hanging Solo . . .

I hate this life so deeply . . . almost as deeply as I wish
I were dead . . .
I intensely hate and dread this life.
Where human value depends,
On wealth you have and is so rife,
With a status image that pretends.

I hate this life so deeply . . . almost as deeply as I wish
I were dead . . .
Suppose you do despise this life
And decide like the Lord, to be poor.
Like lilies of the field live without strife,
Would you still get respect like you had before?

I hate this life so deeply . . . almost as deeply as I wish
I were dead . . .
I would pay a penny for your thought,
Although even that would cost too much.
We struggle to survive with nothing of that sort,
Not even water, food or any such!

I hate this life so deeply . . . almost as deeply as I wish
I were dead . . .
I stare down at the massive, empty plate,
Oh, how I desire someday it will be filled.
Perhaps life will transform according to fate,
At least that way I won't be killed . . .

I hate this life so deeply . . . almost as deeply as I wish
I were dead . . .
Where opinions are wealth,
People aren't concerned about the poor;
They don't bother about our health!
Oh, please, someone, I beg you, aid and cure!

I hate this life so deeply . . . almost as deeply as I wish
I were dead . . .

**Mirali Patel (11)**
**Norbury Manor Business College, Thornton Heath**

## Fears Of A Goth

As I walk through the shadows of darkness,
Blood runs smoothly down my face,
People walking away, looking . . . screaming!
The heavy steps of my long, black boots,
Drench as I walk down the long, windy high street,
I am your thoughts, your nightmares,
The ghost in your attic,
The boogieman under your bed,
The monster in your closet,
I am what they fear, but I mean no harm,
I don't bite (honest!)
I'm just me!
I take deep breaths as people look and stare,
I feel empty, alone! From another planet,
Why can't people accept me?
Why do they keep on asking?
Why don't they just let my long, black coat
Drag behind me?
I am your fears, your tears,
The haunted house,
The full moon,
The crooked trees,
I am a goth,
The goth who's nice,
The goth that respects anyone,
So why can't they respect me?
Your fears are my desire,
I can take the pain away . . . and keep it for myself
I crave the darkness,
So please, please accept me!

**Paris Arnold (13)**
**Norbury Manor Business College, Thornton Heath**

# My Little Daydream

I closed my eyes and pretended I was somewhere else,
Somewhere beautiful and where happiness never ended,
Somewhere where the sun shone and glistened like gold,
Somewhere where the flowers were made of diamonds,
Somewhere where everyone's wishes were granted,

A place where I could find an eternity full of happiness,
A place where I would be loved and cared for,
Where no evil or sadness roamed,
A place where no one would be left out or feel unwanted,
A place where everyone loved and never treated badly,

A place so beautiful that even Mother Nature couldn't invent,
Where even she didn't deserve to be allowed in,
A place where only the good and pure would only be allowed in,
A place where golden butterflies flew through meadows full of gold dust,
A place where trees were made and carved from gold,

Somewhere where gold dust drifted through the air,
A place where people found their true loves,
A place where they found someone they would love forever,
Someone who would never stop loving them, whatever they did,
Someone who would whisper in their ears and tell them they loved them,

I wished I was there and prayed I was there in my little daydream,
My little, made-up place where I wanted to be,
I hoped, when I opened my eyes, I was there, my little daydream,
'Please,' I whispered, 'let me be there,'
I opened my eyes, I was still here, the cold, dark cave,
Alone, by myself, my little daydream gone forever . . .

**Divya Paramasivan (12)**
**Norbury Manor Business College, Thornton Heath**

## Love For All, Hatred For None

Every time I turn on the TV,
The only thing I see is crime,
Why do people waste their time,
Making other people cry?
Crime makes me seriously sad,

They have a family,
What if they got killed?
They have hearts filled with hatred,
How can people become such wild animals?

Just for money,
Why don't you become funny
And make the world laugh?
It's a wonderful world,
Made of shiny gold.

Think about what you're doing,
Before you hold a gun,
That evil thing destroys the fun.

Why not try and find some love?
It's a great feeling,
That helps you peeling
All the hatred out of your heart.

This applies to everyone,
Even all the flies.

Let's fill our hearts with love for all
And hatred for none,
Let's have a world with no more tears,
Let's do all this for no one to have fears.

**Faiza Cheema (13)**
**Norbury Manor Business College, Thornton Heath**

69

# You Are Free

Freedom is your life, freedom is your soul
You don't have freedom, though
You don't have it at all

You live your life regretting,
Regretting what could've been
Could've, would've, should've
And what your eyes have seen

So much anger,
So much constraint,
How did you get here?
Lord, so much restraint

The anger you've experienced,
The verve you deeply lack,
The happiness you commit to,
But it's such a setback

Each day you see the same,
Each hour you pray,
Each minute you ask why,
Each second seems like a delay

But the instant you escape
You know you are freed,
From the life on wheels and chairs,
To the life on clouds and dreams
Carried away, at airspeed,
Forever, ever and ever,
Lord, I am free.

**Kalina Tomova (14)**
**Norbury Manor Business College, Thornton Heath**

## A Special Place

If I could create a place of my imagination,
Built upon my own creation,
Harmony would rule the world
And hatred wouldn't exist to boys and girls.

People would smile and no one would hate,
No arguments, politics, crime or debates,
Teenagers would still survive -
No need to suffer to stay alive.

If everyone tried a little bit more,
We'd find more keys to open the doors
And I do believe there's a place like this,
A place somewhere behind the mist.

So, why can't we live in love and pride?
Instead of living in sadness
In tears that you cry?

A place like this isn't one you can buy,
So it's goodness you need, no anger, nor lies,
I just don't want to hear again on the news,
Another boy killed, injured or bruised.

In a place like mine, this wouldn't happen,
No weirdoes following children to grab them.

In a place like mine
'Bad' isn't tolerated,
Only happiness, something that should be celebrated.

**Megan Lyden (12)**
**Norbury Manor Business College, Thornton Heath**

## Without My Shadow

I can't. I won't.
Let you see.
The pain it has caused me.
All the tears that I cried,
All the times I have sighed,
Not seeing you beside me.

I can't. I won't.
Let you see.
You are the reason for my misery.
You made it worst,
Deadly,
Made it hard to breathe.

I can't. I won't.
Let you see.
I can't live without you,
I care.
That I miss you,
I love you.

I can't. I won't.
Let you see.
My best friend left me
And left me to be me.
You are my soulmate,
You make me complete.

**Chloe Lam (12)**
**Norbury Manor Business College, Thornton Heath**

## Who Am I?

Who am I?

Am I strong?
Am I tall?
Am I everything but small?

Am I Asian or mixed raced
Or something that can't be traced?

I look around, searching for my identity,
Making sure I can find the real me.
A girl whose heart is made of gold,
Whose voice stands out, clear and bold.
A girl who can turn a frown upside down,
But most importantly, a girl who cares for her friends and family.

Trying to blend in with others, changed me forever
And that little voice in my head says, 'Take a bow,'
Making me wish I had never made that mistake now.

Watching people with their friends, family and others,
Makes me miss what I had before:
Someone to be, someone to see, someone that's me.
But now, I'm just another person in the crowd,
But because of this, I can't be proud.

Who am I?

**Rhianne Patel (13)**
**Norbury Manor Business College, Thornton Heath**

73

# Exams

Thirty minutes, start now!
Heart beating
Palms sweating
Head aching
Mouth dry

Twenty minutes to go!
My head pounds
My fists open and close
My pencil feels limp in my hand
Words and numbers scattered across my page

Ten minutes to go!
Pencils scribbling
Huffing and sighing
Page flicking
Feet shuffling

Five minutes to go!
The clock is ticking
I'm still on the first page
My fingers are tingling
The sound of the teachers pacing up and down

Exam over!

**Joelle McKie (14)**
**Norbury Manor Business College, Thornton Heath**

# Friends

There are many people in the world
But the true ones are like the root of a tree
They stay there and support you in your time of need
Hold you up when you are feeling down
But then again, there are the leaves that stay for a few days
Then leave you in distress
But you are my roots, you held me up
When I thought I had a leaf.

**Zalika Ntune (12)**
**Norbury Manor Business College, Thornton Heath**

## A Soldier's Life

*Bang, bang,* is all you hear
You hold onto your gun with fear

Wondering if you'll survive
Trying to be brave when you're sleep deprived

Your family phone and can only cry
You wonder why you did this, why, why, why

Your dream tonight is not good
It's about the dreaded box of wood

You wake up to see your sergeant
Telling you there's news that's urgent

As he tells you, you feel like frost
That's another three men lost

You find some locals surviving on rum
They're actually Taliban with a gun

Oh, my goodness, we won the war
Time to go home and celebrate
Victory galore!

**Chloe Ballard (13)**
**Norbury Manor Business College, Thornton Heath**


## The World Around Us!

We are all so different
Unique in every way
Born poor or rich
Black or white
Gender or race
Culture or background
Religion neither faith, was judged of us
Supposedly we loved the people we are.

What would the world around us
That we live in have been like?

**Bahja Mussa (12)**
**Norbury Manor Business College, Thornton Heath**

**75**

## The Night's Show

They fly through the starry night
Resembling streams of colourful kites
For the young, the old, the rich, the poor
A dream for each, for each fly through the door.

They settle in a person's mind
And play the dream
That took so long to write.

Each dream is different
Each one unique
Some are defined and some are bleak.

When dawn breaks
They leave their hosts
Their circle, they fly
Way up high
But they're immortal
They never die.

So, up to the heavens they go
To prepare for the next night's show.

**Zahra Ladha (12)**
**Norbury Manor Business College, Thornton Heath**

## Autumn

When the mornings are chilly
And skies are blue,
I hear birds singing old and new,
All snug in their nests,
Or flying up high,
I believe I see a hint of red in the sky,
All in their shells
And piled in a heap,
I find some conkers good to keep,
All shiny and smooth
And very soft I must include.
I can almost taste fresh bread
And soup drifting through the air,
It tastes like happiness, joy and laughter,
Never anger, sorrow or despair
And that is how I must compare
And finally, I smell a new day,
A new chance, a new season

And a clean slate.

**Emma Miller (12)**
**Norbury Manor Business College, Thornton Heath**

## In Hiding

A secret hidden
The truth forbidden
You hide away
From light's glowing ray

A secret hidden
The truth forbidden
In the shadows you hide
From the world outside

A secret hidden
The truth forbidden
Divided from the crowd
Outside not allowed

A secret hidden
The truth forbidden
The silent crying
Of you, in hiding.

**Hannan Boakye (12)**
**Norbury Manor Business College, Thornton Heath**


## The Spirit

Every night when the clock strikes twelve,
I look out the window and see her there,
I never actually see her face, but she's dark,
She's tall and she's fierce,
She looks evil, because she's surrounded by darkness,
But I see through the image she portrays,
I know this, because she's helped a mouse,
Who was about to be turned into dinner,
She -
*Ding-dong!*
The clock strikes twelve-thirty, *poof!*
She's gone without a trace,
Like she was never there.

**Hajar Zarrai (12)**
**Norbury Manor Business College, Thornton Heath**

## My Timeless Existence

I don't wait around for you to catch up
I slip past you all the time, but you never notice
I live immortally, with none of my kind
I drift along the Earth's crust, brushing away the past.

You measure me with gadgets, but I outrun your scales
You let me lead you through life
As if you are an inexperienced child
Clinging onto my timeless existence
To guide you through the days.

My hands are dated, frail and weak
But this job that I'm tied to, can only be done by me
For I am the only one of my eternal kind
No matter how much it hurts me, I have to carry on.

I will be remembered for as long as I live
And as long as that may be
I will never die.

**Maimuna Khan (14)**
**Norbury Manor Business College, Thornton Heath**

## Art Is What I Do

The thing I like best, is art
I'm not dumb, but not smart
Art runs in the family, I guess
Sometimes it comes out a mess

I always try to do my best
I put my brain to the test
Sometimes I do it for fun
Drawing the red-hot sun

I always keep on trying
I'm always sighing
Art is what I do
To me, it's so true.

**Sarita Wagay (13)**
**Norbury Manor Business College, Thornton Heath**

**79**

## Pursue Your Dreams

Your dreams are high
And you want them to fly,
But someone knocks you down
And then you frown.
But don't be a clown,
There's no need to frown,
Shout your dreams out loud.

Your dreams are high
And you want them to fly,
If you work hard,
They will write you a card,
Saying your dream has come true,
If you pursue,
Your dreams will come true
And it's all down to you,
Shout your dreams out loud!

**Georgia Jones (13)**
**Norbury Manor Business College, Thornton Heath**


## Youth Of Today

I have an armour every day of my life
Because I'm scared to get threatened with a knife.

I feel when old ladies run from me
They probably think they're going to get beat.

When we're in a group, they think it's a gang
Because most of the time we wear black bandana bands.

All they need to do, is get to know us,
Before they come and stereotype us!

We are not horrible and not hooligans,
But their idea of us is like an illusion.

My message to you, adults of today, is please give us a chance
And a glance!

**Anieshka Onze Mido (13)**
**Norbury Manor Business College, Thornton Heath**

80

# I Am Who I Am!

Maybe you don't like me, maybe you hate me
But I am who I am and I'm not going to change for you!
You might think I'm ugly or even meek
But I am who I am and I'm not going to change for you!
You look at my face, as if I'm a disgrace
But I don't care, I am who I am
The world is missed with different faces,
People judging the wrong thing
It's time to stop and look how the world is changing
Because we are who we are
You are who you are
Because you're unique and amazing
Everyone has their own personality
You are who you are
Because God has made you that way
Be grateful, because you are who you are.

**Tamera Kanon (13)**
**Norbury Manor Business College, Thornton Heath**

# Dad

Dad, oh Dad, you make me feel so sad
Why do you smoke if you know it's so bad?
You are so close to me, I don't want to lose you
You mean so much to me, even though I fool you
Dad, oh Dad, I love you so much.

Please try to understand,
I want to say that you are banned,
But what can I do?
You are my dad!
Dad, oh Dad,
You make me feel so sad.

Dad, oh Dad,
I love you so much.

**Fatima Hussain (13)**
**Norbury Manor Business College, Thornton Heath**

**81**

# I Am Who I Am

I am proud to be me,
I want everyone to know,
I am proud to be me,
I want everyone to see,
That I am who I am
And I'm not gonna change,
I am who I am,
I won't rearrange,
At times I stop
And wonder to myself,
At times I stop,
To think of myself,
I don't really care,
What people have to say,
I am who I am,
Each and every day.

**Flavia Small (13)**
**Norbury Manor Business College, Thornton Heath**

## What Are Friends?

What are friends?
Friends are there to be there for you
When times are hard and you need comfort.
What are friends?
Friends should give you confidence
Not keep you down.
What are friends?
Friends don't stop you from living your dream
They persuade you to go on.
Are you a friend?
Yes, you are a friend, because you're there
When I need you and let me live life.

**Selina Osei-Bonsu (12)**
**Norbury Manor Business College, Thornton Heath**

# He

Life is tough
And the ride is rough.
It is incredibly hard,
Though we put on a facade.
Yet He certainly knows,
That it is all hoaxes and shows.
He gets how we feel,
With knowledge, so real.
He sees our thoughts and He sees our soul,
He sees a gap and He fills that hole.
He searches our heart, He fulfils our desire,
He loves us so much, like red burning fire.
He holds us so tight,
He's our bright shining light.
He does us a favour,
By being our Saviour.

**Rachel Billington (12)**
**Norbury Manor Business College, Thornton Heath**

## No Guns, No Knives

No guns, no knives
It kills people's lives
It's dangerous, it's wrong
Why don't we get along?
Crime everywhere
It makes us stop in fear
Keeping us hostage at home
It makes it harder to roam
Seeing gangs on streets
Brings the tension and the heat
No knives, no guns
Let's all enjoy and have fun.

**Abigail Walters (13)**
**Norbury Manor Business College, Thornton Heath**

# Family

A family is a group of people closest to each other
They can be a bother, but they are always there for each other.

A mother is someone who bosses you around
And screams at every sound
She tries to act cool, but she just doesn't rule.

A sister is someone who brings you shame and calls you lame
Someone who will steal, but the love between you will never heal
You know she loves you, even though she shoves you.

A dad is someone who is never around
But treats you like a princess and gives you a crown
He jokes around and says, 'Don't be impolite,' and works all day and
night.

A brother is someone who thinks he's the best
But trust me, he's just like the rest.

**Aida Hassan (12)**
**Norbury Manor Business College, Thornton Heath**

## The Final Goal

Blood, sweat and tears,
All worth it as the crowd cheers.
The final strike,
The final goal.
The surge of the net,
The fans with the winning bet.
The celebration flip,
The dive into the crowd.
As the final whistle blows,
I am so proud.
I jump up and down,
Shouting and screaming.
I look at the cup,
It's bright and gleaming.
My team and I are elated,
The other team frustrated.
The tension grows,
As I lift the cup.
The streamers fall down,
The other team frown.
The fireworks discharge,
My happiness at large.
The crowd roars and cheers
And I burst into tears.

As I dream and think,
That that could be me.
But I have to go now,
My mum says it's tea.

**Adam Meineck (13)**
**Oriel High School, Crawley**

## Destiny Of A Feather:

A feather is light;
A wind-caught object in which the gentle twisting knots of wind
Push it back and forth,
As if it were a tide of waves.
Like a wandering spirit, it travels across many different terrains,
As if it were lost on the never-ending path of life.

As a feather scarpers, it passes over many lands and skies dark and blue,
Over trees, dark, golden-reds, earth dry and cold,
It spirals past everything,
Watching age swallow the creeping stroll of life,
Time flows through its ghostly white frond,
But it does not decay, nor become lost,
Because everything and everyone has a destiny,
Even when you are aging, you never become old,
Until you find your purpose, your self-being.

Until you find yourself, you're immortality will stay forever,
As though it were a tree standing firm for thousands of years,
So when a feather finally lays to rest with its destiny,
It has found its true owner,
You and your link between feather and man,
Represent the soul of the inner being,
Just like a caterpillar cocooning and thrusting
Its beauties upon the world,
The morphing transformation is the border
Between boy and man,
Or immaturity and maturity!

**Kershaw Lawrence (16)**
**Philpots Manor School, West Hoathly**

## Him

Ah, he is coming closer
And closer.
His eyes lock me in place,
I don't know what to do.
I start to hyperventilate,
I stare back at him;
I stare at his gorgeous body;
I stare at his beautiful hair;
I stare at his deep crystal-like eyes.
That's where my eyes stay;
His eyes,
I can see his soul,
His pure, selfless, charming soul.
But do you know what the best part is . . . ?
He is mine.

**Claudia Dominguez (13)**
**Redruth School, Redruth**

## Roses And Me

Grown from a seed, like a life from a spark,
The droop of a petal, like the beat of a heart.
The sharpness of thorns, like the sting of cruel speech,
The lifting of leaves, like a hug within reach.

Leaning towards the sun, like the fear of no light,
The touch of the earth, like a kiss from the night.
The welcome of rain, like a tear from the sea,
Similar we are, roses and me.

**Chelsea Rose Fowler (13)**
**Redruth School, Redruth**

## The World

This world is great
Even though I came late
I don't know why I started to cry
How and why will I die?
The slap on the butt was a bullet
That was how I entered this.

When I was walking it was so awesome
I'm just very worried I will be dumb
My mummy's arms were grabbing me
The buzzing and stinging of a bee
Very much exasperates me
This is how my toddler years began.

Going to school is very boring
Working, answering and mind-numbing
*Boom, crash* and *smash* goes the kid
I'm even copying what he did
I can't wait to become a dad
This is how my childhood began.

Finally, I'm in secondary school
Still trying to act very cool
Getting up at 6am and taking the bus
My mum says I'm growing too fast
And I must be much more responsible
This is my life up to now!

**Joseph Adusei (12)**
**St Joseph's College, London**

**88**

## Predator

The bubbles I made slowly float up
And my friends shroud my favourite bed of coral
As I fly through this wet sky
I keep my eyes sharp for any predators stalking me.

The waves slowly come to a halt
My senses tell me to run away
I cannot do this
For the predator has struck me still.

When I start to flap my tail wings
My mind becomes addicted to this thrill
*Snap, snap,* I hear and start to dash along
But before I could get away, the shark sings his sweet song.

'Little fish . . .' it moans
'I only want to play . . .'
'Leave me alone!' I shout
'I've had a bad day!'

I slowly turn to slip away
But the shark opens its jaws
And fastening on my bones
Those white spikes gnaw!

**Bradley McElroy (12)**
**St Joseph's College, London**

## Eyes Of Violence

I lay in the cradle, lying with nothing to hold,
I see everyone smiling, I am one day old.

I sat there writing, writing as told,
This makes no sense, I am five years old.

I sat there riding, riding in the cold,
I looked back worried, I am ten years old.

I crouched there staring, staring at the gold,
I want it so much, I am fifteen years old.

I stood there punching, punching at his face,
I know it is wrong, for I am a disgrace.

I lay there crying, crying at my error,
I know about violence, believe me, it is a terror.

Violence or peace? Which should I choose?
For violence is nature, waiting to come loose.

Peace is self-control, something I must gain,
I have eyes of violence; this would remain as a stain.

**Vignesh Sivan (13)**
**St Joseph's College, London**


## The Eight-Legged Stranger

The eight-legged stranger spins a web of mystery
To capture an unfortunate bug
And put it out of its misery
As the eight-legged stranger feeds
Come summer, go summer, winter is upon us
It's morning and the eight-legged stranger's web
Is laden with beads.

Come winter, go winter, spring is upon us
The eight-legged stranger lays her children
Scattered across the Earth
As she passes away.

**Tomi Fayefunmi (12)**
**St Joseph's College, London**

## Bulldog Clip

His owner presses down on his legs
And his mouth opens wide,
His owner takes two pieces of paper
And shoves them inside.

The bulldog clip stands strong on the table,
His victims in his iron jaw,
The wind tries to free the condemned paper,
But the bulldog fights back even more.

He stands there for hours,
Then his owner finally returns,
But then a sad, sad lesson,
Poor bulldog clip finally learns;

He stands guard for ages,
New challenges he may meet,
He waits for his owner's return,
But does not receive a treat!

**Luke Burns (12)**
**St Joseph's College, London**

## The Eyes

The eyes kept watching me,
In the shadows in the light,
In the darkness of the night.

Always there, watching me,
What do they need to see?
Deep depths of the sea,
Is the colour of these eyes.

Behind these eyes, darkness lurks
How they glare,
How they stare,
Watching me.

Oh what, oh what, do they need to see?

**Cialan Browne (12)**
**St Joseph's College, London**

**91**

# Summer Sun

The summer sun, our friend to seeds
And plants and to all life
In temperate climates meets our needs
And gives us hope that succeeds

In tropic places, the sun will burn
And turn the land to desert sand
Crack open Earth and take the lives
Of people, cattle and all hope

Sun is life and sun is death
And sun is hope and sun is despair
Sun is summer and green, green growth
Or sun is silence and bleached bones.

**Damian Balasubramanam (11)**
**St Joseph's College, London**

# The Life Of Seashores

The sea wakes
The sun shines
The sand glows
The wind blows

The sea flows
The sun boils
The sand spoils
The wind whistles

The sea shakes
The sun wakes
The sand bakes
The wind sleeps.

**Vithushan Jeyapahan (12)**
**St Joseph's College, London**

## The River Of Life

The gentle current taking me down
All is fine
All is good
Safe and sound
The river bears me
Onward towards the end

Downstream I feel the river beneath me
Gathering speed
The current gains a sense of urgency
Can I stop? Should I stop?

Faster, faster
I want to abort
Calming me the current slows
Then rushing on again
Danger foams ahead
I scream for it to stop
But it won't listen

Time slows down
The angry waters of danger
Boil and heave around me
I scream for it to stop
But stop it will not

I see it for a second
Then *bam,* straight in the face
Pain, anguish, guilt
Afterwards all is lost
Except one thing
My face

The river of life goes on
Even though I'm different now
The people of the river hurry on
Or stop, stare
But life still goes on.

**Matthew Rendell (13)**
**St Peter's CE Aided School, Exeter**

93

## Facialist

I look out of my eyes
At least they're the same.
They're the only part of me
That doesn't feel pain.

My face is disfigured
And my arms are scarred.
I just want my old life back
But I'm well and truly barred.

I know I'm not dead
But it's still not the same.
Everyone stares at me
Like I'm grease or a stain.

I can feel people stare
As I walk by.
I hold up my head
And try not to cry.

I look out of my eyes
Now I know they're the same.
This is forever
Forever is pain.

**Katie Woolacott (13)**
**St Peter's CE Aided School, Exeter**

## Facialist

Don't look at me like I'm a freak
Don't treat me like I'm stupid, or worse - weak
Now that you've seen my face, you'll never look at me the same
But I'm not an animal that you can tame
If I could, I'd break all the mirrors in the world
I would change my face, I'd do it if I could
When I look at my reflection, I know I'll never look the same
But all I want is to be me again . . .

**Shaianne Barnes (13)**
**St Peter's CE Aided School, Exeter**

# I Know

I know I'm kind of different
I know I might be strange
I know I'm not so likeable
I know I'm not the same

But I am not an alien
I'm not from outer space
I am an ordinary person
It's just because of my face

I know I'm kind of different
I know I might be strange
I know I'm not so likeable
I know I'm not the same

I know I have some problems
But it is not so bad
I don't care what you guys think
Because deep down, I'm not sad

I know I'm kind of different
I know I might be strange
I know I'm not so likeable
I know I'm not the same.

**Henry Ruane (13)**
**St Peter's CE Aided School, Exeter**

# The Facialist

Look at him there, staring at the floor,
We don't like him, he looks a bore,
We bully him once,
We bully him twice,
We bully him thrice,
'Cause we're not very nice.

**Ryan Cassidy (13)**
**St Peter's CE Aided School, Exeter**

## Facialist

I went to ASDA,
To get some tea
And this old dude,
Came and crippled me.

He said,

'Roses are red,
Violets are blue,
Your face is messed up
And so are you.'

He said,

'When I went to ASDA,
For a cup of tea,
These chavs came along
And took the mick out of me.'

He said,

'Roses are red,
Violets are blue,
You're a munter,
Coz you look like a loo.'

**Max Wenley (12)**
**St Peter's CE Aided School, Exeter**


## Facialist

I am fat, I am round,
People bounce me up and down.

I'm only a man,
But no one understands that I got hit by a van.

I am special, I am cool,
People beat me up at school.

My face is messed up,
All my friends are dressed up ducks.

**George Kenworthy (13)**
**St Peter's CE Aided School, Exeter**

## Facialist

The guilt in his eyes is like an unreflective mirror -
Reminding me of what he can now see
The inquisitive look on his face stabs me.

The disappointment inside me pushes a tear
Hopefully to remind him that I am still here.

Does he know what it feels like?
Does he know my pain?
Does he know what it feels like
To know that I will never walk again?

I thought he would understand
I thought he would see
I thought he would see that I am still me!

But obviously not
He doesn't care
So why should I sit here and let him stare?

So I break his gaze
And leave him there.

**Holly Price (13)**
**St Peter's CE Aided School, Exeter**

## Facialist

Amazed, interested and disgusted,
But if you make a remark, you'll get busted.

Yes, I may be messed up,
But at least I didn't get locked up.

I am lonely and I do get mocked,
But being different really rocks.

If you're in my shoes for a day,
But maybe you'll just understand, OK?

I am different coz I have a dog's face,
But I have a life that you can't trace.

**Harvey Ridgeway (13)**
**St Peter's CE Aided School, Exeter**

**97**

# Facialist Poem

I act like I don't care
When people in the street look and stare
I try hard to put on a face
As I'm walking down the street at a very fast pace.

I'm only a man
But people just don't understand
How it makes me feel when they mock me
I just don't know what they see.

Last night, I had a flashback
It's as if my world has turned black
I walk to school on my own
With no friends, I feel so alone.

I feel like everybody's playing games, tricks
In their own little cliques
I feel like I'm always pretending
Like my life is never-ending . . .

And it is all because of that accident that happened last weekend . . .

**Ella Hazelton (13)**
**St Peter's CE Aided School, Exeter**

## Facialist Poem

It was one night, one mistake
And I'm left with this scar on my face.
I try not to take it to heart,
But when they look and laugh,
I can't stand the shame,
They put on my face again.
They make me feel like it's my fault,
I didn't ask for this to happen,
If it was my choice . . .
This wouldn't be the way . . .

I can't bear the way things have changed,
My life's turned upside down.
When I walk into a room, everyone stares,
It used to be because I was the main man there,
But now it's because of my face.
They make me feel like I've changed,
But I'm still here,
Me! Me! Me!

**Grace Carter (13)**
**St Peter's CE Aided School, Exeter**

## Facialist

With everyone there, staring at me,
I am the centre of attention,
I try really hard not to be,
But I have no protection,
I'm the one with the weird face,
With burns all around,
I used to be invisible,
Now I'm the most popular kid in town!

I wouldn't choose this for anyone,
I just wish people could see,
I don't want my dad thinking weird of his son,
I don't even wanna be me!

**Chloe Andrews (13)**
**St Peter's CE Aided School, Exeter**

**99**

## Facialist

I try and build up my courage,
Ready to go to school,
Not sure if I can make it,
Without losing my cool.

I walk into the classroom,
With my head held high,
But everyone turns around
And I wish I could die.

Everything has changed,
I have to put on an act,
I try and erase that memory,
Even though it's a fact.

I eventually get home,
I try hard not to cry,
I look into the mirror
And I know I have to try.

**Mia Pang (13)**
**St Peter's CE Aided School, Exeter**

## Facialist

Do you know what it feels like
When you can't be normal?
You can't be sane
People think you're not the same.

Well, if you got to know me
If you started to care
You would know
That it I cannot bare.

So, if you stop on the street
And stare at me
Just think what I go through
And have some sympathy.

**Louis Domville-Musters (13)**
**St Peter's CE Aided School, Exeter**

## Facialist

Just because my face is gone,
Doesn't mean my soul has too.

Whenever I go into a public place,
People scatter all over the place.

People act like I'm different,
Even though I'm the same within.

I sometimes feel like I'm an alien,
Stranded a million miles away.

When I go to bed,
I hope I don't wake up
And die a simple death.

I am just normal, but no one understands,
It's not my fault I'm different,
I'm different than the rest of the crowd.

**William Roberts (13)**
**St Peter's CE Aided School, Exeter**

## Face

When I look at you
You look at me too
I feel left out
Without a doubt
I am the same inside

Looking at me
I am looking at you
This pair of eyes
That I can't hide from

I want to be the same
But all I feel is lame
When I'm feeling blue
Because you're looking at me too.

**Zara Emily Thurgood (13)**
**St Peter's CE Aided School, Exeter**

# Face And Feelings

If you see me in the street
Why stop and stare?

I used to be like you and I wouldn't care
Why don't you crack a joke?
It's all people do!
Maybe if you got to know me
You would realise I am a lot like you!

I don't get many chances to prove myself and shine
It's just really hard to avoid the staring faces all the time.

It's just a lot more difficult for me
Or that is what people say.

But I really want people to know I am not strange
But most people won't ever know
I'm not some kind of walking freak show.

**Joe McCrea Smith (13)**
**St Peter's CE Aided School, Exeter**

# Just Because Of The Way I Look

I stare up to see this giant
So big, so tall
But they don't know what I've been through
I'm scared
I'm frightened
I can't look up
I am stuck in a corner from which I can't get up

Just because of the way I look
You treat me so bad
I feel so sad
I wish I could change this
I don't understand
Please help me

Please do!

**Jack Hoskins (12)**
**St Peter's CE Aided School, Exeter**

## My Best Friend

When you leave, I will always remember,
Our smiles shared,
Our big hugs,
Our hyper moments.

When you leave, it won't be the same,
No one to look up to,
To ask for advice,
To share all my worries with.

When you leave, I will always remember,
Our never-ending giggles,
Our secret jokes,
Only meant for us to understand.

When you leave, I won't be complete,
You're my other half,
I share everything with you,
Without you I'm lost.

When you leave, I will always remember,
The times you've been there,
A shoulder for me to cry on,
You wipe my tears away.

When you leave, my life will change forever,
I will be thrown into the deep end,
Forced to find my own way,
To face the world alone.

When you leave, I will always remember you,
My best friend!
You will stay in my heart forever,
Our memories never lost.

**Beth Milverton (14)**
**St Wilfrid's School, Exeter**

# The Satisfaction Of Man

Nature is built with balance,
Sun feeds the plants,
Plants feed the animals,
Animals feed the killers.

Society is built with hunger
That eats and eats,
And takes and takes
Until the grass turns yellow and the sky turns black . . .

Man is built with greed
That makes his thoughts bleed.
Till he steps back
And sees that there is nothing left.

Regret is built with sadness,
It seeds undoing wrongs,
And is the first step
Towards something new.

But such is the passage of time,
Too fast to fold
And time will always be the one thing
We can't hold . . .

This is not a prophecy,
This is not a foretelling,
This is not an entertaining prose,
This is the will of the world.

**Theo Lezzeri (13)**
**St Wilfrid's School, Exeter**

## The Cat That Hunts In The Night

It's not a door,
Or a dripping of a tap -
It's the flipping and flapping
Of the cat's door flap.

He is on a mission,
To find a treat,
Something he will be sure to eat.

The way he walks,
The way he cries,
The way the moon reflects his eyes.

He will jump, dive, pounce and crawl,
To get a prize he will adore,
After this, it's pure bliss,
For the cat that hunts in the night.

Like a bullet through the flap,
It's time for a nap,
For the cat that hunts in the night.

**Brianna Miller (11)**
**St Wilfrid's School, Exeter**


## Boxes

I like boxes
They can be expensive
Or can be cheap.
You can buy them in shops
If they are waterproof
You can put water in them.
Boxes are cool.
You can store stuff in them.
They can be hollow or solid.

**Elliot Dawson (11)**
**St Wilfrid's School, Exeter**

**105**

## Life Shall Never Be The Same

I'm going to miss them.
My whole life wrapped around them like a woolly scarf,
Keeping each other safe.
From the baby's cot, to the big bed, to school on to further education,
We have all been through it together, the good times and the bad times.
It's never been easy, living with brothers that can't understand you.
If I could, I would give my life to them.
When anyone thinks about laying a finger on them,
I'm always there to stand up for them, as I am their protection.
Life has been so hard, the arguments, the tears, the shouting.
But now the time has come.
All will be quiet, the feeling shall be odd,
Wondering what will happen next in my life.
I shall miss them, but at least I have all the memories,
They are right here, kept locked in my heart.
Life shall never be the same without them.

**Tessa Harvey (14)**
**St Wilfrid's School, Exeter**

## Flowers

Flowers! You see them everywhere
And can't help but stop and stare.
Such beauty, such colour,
So wonderful, so pick them for your mother!
Slowly they grow,
Slowly they flower,
Watch them develop with all that power.
Some grow big,
Others grow small,
They are truly so colourful.
Flowers on the ground,
Flowers in the trees,
They all make a home for the happy, buzzing bees!

**Jack Goddard (14)**
**St Wilfrid's School, Exeter**

## Friends And Family

F riends are great to share secrets,
R emember they cheer you when you're sad
I think my friends are the best,
E very one of them is loyal to me.
N ot all the time we get along, but we
D o always make up again.
S hopping, bowling or the cinema

A re great places to hang out.
N umerous fun times we have had together,
D ancing is something we love to do.

F amily are great to talk to,
A nd they never let you down.
M y family support and help me,
I n every way they can.
L ots of fights happen between us,
Y et we still love each other.

**Danielle Dutton (13)**
**St Wilfrid's School, Exeter**


## Food Or Drink?

F oods can be dry or juicy
O f all, pizza is the best!
O ccasionally, foods can be deadly -
D efinitely wouldn't eat goat's eyeballs!

A niseed ice cream sticks in my throat!
N ightmare curry keeps you awake at night!
D readful slimy snakes are tasty no doubt!

D rinks are thirst-quenching and fun!
R emember to drink water every day -
I f you do, you won't fade away!
N ow consider carefully what you
K now about wonderful food and drink.

**James Dutton (12)**
**St Wilfrid's School, Exeter**

107

## Life Has Rewards

L ife is given to us all
I think it best that we obey each rule
F ood and drink fuel our heart
E verything in the world is a unique piece of art

H and in hand we live each day
A s the sun beats down ray by ray
S un shining in a magnificent way

R ainbows arching across the sky
E veryone asking the question why
W hy were we given this glorious life?
A s for the answer, we may never know
R eality as answers are hard to find
D espite this, I don't really mind
S ince life's full of amazing rewards.

**Ben Snow (14)**
**St Wilfrid's School, Exeter**

## Cupcakes

Cupcakes are sticky and sweet,
Decorated all so neat,
Coloured icing plopped on top,
Good enough to buy in a shop.

Pink icing so girly,
Blue icing so swirly,
Gold icing very neat,
Multicoloured icing very sweet.

Decorated they look great,
What about one for a good mate?
I think cupcakes are the best cake,
And they are easy to make!

**Emily Semmens (12)**
**St Wilfrid's School, Exeter**

**108**

## The Desert

The blinding sun bakes down onto the ground,
As if there is no life around,
The heat of the sand hurts our feet,
This place is called the desert.

Whatever still lives there,
Isn't affected by the boiling air,
The bones of animals scatter the earth,
The snakes and lizards have slender girths.

The desert is vicious to all living things,
Even to birds who spread their wings,
The strong winds pick up sand and whistle,
When they destroy . . . every living being.

**Matthew Semmens (13)**
**St Wilfrid's School, Exeter**


## The Darkness

In go the men, the bringers of fear
Looking in corners, the darkness is near
They can hear snakes but only men are near
As they move out the darkness is there

*Bang!* goes a car, man on the ground
Smoke all around, nowhere to go
Run to the house and lock all the doors
Onto the roof, closer to their destination

No use in firing, the darkness is there
Hide in the smoke till the extraction is near
They jump to a wall which feels like a fort
'I can hear my saviour, he's here, he's . . .'

No use in helping, they're dead to me
Sent out some men to get them for me
I'll phone the family, tell them he fought bravely
Get me a drink, I am rather thirsty.

**Najim Al-Baghdadi (14)**
**Seaford College, Petworth**

**109**

# The Television Guide
### *(To the tune of 'Fireflies' by Owl City)*

A magical, wondrous thing,
Projecting the imaging
Of some kids TV as we eat at dawn.

By nine I can watch no more -
Daytime TV: what a bore!
It is just a massive Corrie omnibus.

By four it has upped its game:
No more 'Bargain Hunt' in this frame.
Four pm is when all the good stuff starts.

I have to force myself to read
The daily paper's headlines.
You can't believe a word they say:
It's all a load of lies.
But that is all that you will ever find -
Keep that in mind.

I like watching 'Dragon's Den'
And classical 'Bill and Ben' -
I can't wait 'til ten
Cos that's when the news is on.

On Friday was my favourite show,
But it's ended now - what a blow.
I'll just have to wait for old Johnnie Ross.

The night screen's at 2am,
But there's not much on by then -
I'll just have to sleep 'til six
When it starts again.

I have to force myself to read
The daily paper's headlines.
You can't believe a word they say:
It's all a load of lies.
But that is all that you will ever find -
Keep that in mind.

**Alex MacPherson (14)**
**Seaford College, Petworth**

## A Lover's Tale

'Where has Rose gone, Florence?
Where has Rose gone?
I went upstairs to find her, Florence,
For her I do so long.

Tomorrow we should have been wed,
Till death do us part,
Now that she has gone, Florence,
She has broken my heart.

Why do you cry, Florence
When I say her name?
Where has she gone, Florence
And is she is pain?

'Oh, Rose was such a beauty
So good and fair was she.'
'What are you saying, Florence?
Why do you say was to me?'

'Oh, Rose is dead now, Jethro,
Yes, she is dead and gone,
So you can be with me now,
You know I am the one.'

'Oh no, it is Rose that I adore,
She's the one I love,
What is that you hold in your hand?
Is it her purple glove?

And what's that I see upon it?
It looks like blood to me.
Tell me where she is, Florence
And do not lie to me.'

'I am her killer, Jethro, I know it was wrong,
You two were not meant to be.
Please, I love you Jethro, I am the one,
Oh Jethro, can't you see?'

**Ellie Kleinlercher (11)**
**Seaford College, Petworth**

**111**

## The House

In the house there was a room,
In the room there was a wall,
On the wall there was a broom,
Behind the broom was a hall,
For only one little creature, known as the mouse.

The mouse was small, but very smart,
She wore a white pinny,
In which she liked to draw art.
To us it's really quite mini,
But it's the right size for a mouse.

Each year on the 1st of May,
The mouse, known as Maisy Maureen,
Knew it was time for a trip away,
Because today was the spring clean.
She went to pick raspberries for a sweet little mouse.

She gathered enough,
To watch the children play
And she walked home on the tough,
Because she was here to stay.
The spring clean had stopped, not aware of the mouse.

She said proudly, 'Let the summer begin!'
But something else was born.
The landlord burst right in
And said, 'You must be gone!'
So she packed up and left,
Which was strange for a mouse.

In the house there was a room,
In the room there was a wall,
On the wall there was a broom,
Behind the broom there was a hall,
Where once a little creature lived,
Known as the mouse.

**Jenny Kent (13)**
**Seaford College, Petworth**

## Dictionary
*(To the tune of 'Fireflies' by Owl City)*

It's filled with a thousand words
Anything from trees to birds
It looks a bore but that's ignorance,
It takes up half a shelf
No room to have a twelfth
But that's OK because it's all you need

I'm going to force myself to read
To find out
What
That
Word
Means
I know it now it's all OK
Until another day
Can't wait to skim through letters A to K.

Nouns, verbs and adjectives
Trying to find where that word lives
Something I don't know, I'm really stuck
The Oxford edition's great
It's almost like a mate
It shows me the way to certain unknown words.

I'm going to force myself to read
To find out
What
That
Word
Means
I know it now it's all OK
Until another day
Can't wait to skim through letters A to K.
A to K . . .

**Oliver Gatland (14)**
**Seaford College, Petworth**

**113**

# The Pond

I was walking home late from school,
I had an awful day, bullied by all,
A car screeched along down a road,
I reluctantly trudged on as if carrying a load.

I came to a wood, what more could go wrong?
So I walked straight in, noticing a stagnant pong.
I followed the smell and came to a pond,
It was old and sad, no living bond.

I leant over to see inside,
I saw a dead cat that had fallen in and died.
Then I saw the skull of a dog,
Then the wings and the arms of a bird and a frog.

I started to turn then *screech* went an owl,
I jumped back then heard a wolf howl,
I fell in the pond, it was cold and sticky,
I went to get out, I tried, it was tricky.

I was stuck, like a fly in a web when the spider is near,
I tried not to think, but I knew death was here.
How long till I was dragged under to eventually die?
I closed my eyes and started to cry.

I held my breath, how long would I wait,
Until I eventually died and met my fate?
Then I heard a noise not far away,
Would I live to see another day?

It was a man, quite tall, with a happy face,
He had a fish in his hand, maybe a plaice.
'Help!' I screamed, he threw a rope,
He pulled me out, I thanked my hope.

I was walking home late from school,
I had an adventurous day, but scary for all.

**Theo Ormrod Davis (13)**
**Seaford College, Petworth**

## Wolf

My paws crunched on the crisp snow,
My nose twitched letting me know.
Halfway up the hill, a group of elk,
Time to call for the others' help.

As I howled, I listened too,
The elk were anxious as they moved through.
They knew my pack was here to stay,
Waiting for just one to stray.

I waited, patient, for my pack to come,
So we could take down just that one.
The pups would munch most of it
And we'd be left with scraps to eat.

The pack was there, it was time to fight,
I felt like I was twice my height.
We set our sights on one of few,
To feed the pack, we'd need two.

After this we'd hunt again,
Else we would get hunger pains.
I would do what I could
To give them a helping hand.

The hunt began,
I ran from the wings,
We were using the ambush attack,
We worked well as a pack.

The hunt went well,
A feast from Hell.
The pups gathered around
With barely a sound.

**Ellen Gowers (13)**
**Seaford College, Petworth**

# Badgered

There was a house, tall for its place,
Deep in the jungle of the neighbourhood,
Badgered by badgers in every case.
'Come and see,' she said, in a good mood,
But that, that was at the start.

They clawed right through the fence,
And nibbled around the wire,
Like a chainsaw without any sense,
'Please stop it,' she said with fire,
But that, that was at the beginning.

They had tried all the traps and more,
But they still came back with revenge,
They had destroyed the garden with claws,
'This is a nightmare,' she said through the 'fence',
But that, that wasn't the end.

They tunnelled down into the cellar,
Clawed frantically at the bricks,
Until all that was left was a pillar,
'We're homeless,' she said in a flick,
But that, that was nearly over.

There was some land, small for its place,
Deep in the jungle of a ghost town,
Destroyed by badgers in every case.
And she came back with a frown,
But that, that was at the end.

**Oliver Parkes (14)**
**Seaford College, Petworth**

## The Research Scientist

With His measuring cups He separates time's impurities,
With His plastic spoons He does pretend to taste life's
voluptuousness,
With His silver scoops He tenderly selects the steel-blue surmised
joys,
With His forceps He extracts hearts in despair to analyse
                    The spring of our spiritual deaths.

With His old scalpel He dissects ourselves to see if the warm liquor
    Of immortality seeps through our cold-blooded veins - no pain,
With His sharp blades and silver knives He travels through our
minds,
With his optical microscopes He is in search of our souls,
    As we demand to see what could only be sensed,
    Perceive the world through magnifying lens,
With His forensic syringes He steals tormented thoughts
    From fated patients of evanescent life.

With His pipettes He tries to cease fugitive vapours of faith,
With the supreme price in His viridian ampoules He guards
                    Presumed secrets of the eternal life,
With His test tubes He mixes twin lives in a flask,
While we take His pastilles - escape the artificial reality of our lives.

And as He still stirs the cobalt-blue liquid of peace,
It alters into a red liquid - more attractive to our world.
The drops of time meander on the cylindrical vessels
And wrinkle our pain while our pulses still drown away.

**Veronica Guranda (17)**
**Seaford College, Petworth**

# The Door

The door stands tall and proud
In the shabby little house, never opened.
Many have tried but none prevail,
So, it's forgotten and left to rot.

I've never forgotten, that tall oak door,
That stands so indifferently upon the oak floor,
Many a thing could be beyond . . .
But I will never know.

Maybe a kingdom full of creatures that fly
Through mountains of gold and rivers of dreams
The velvet sky glinting with pleasure . . .
I will never know.

Maybe even a wood with odd-looking trees
That twist and turn, this way and that,
Roots creeping across the leaf-strewn floor . . .
I will never know.

Or even a hall holding a grand-looking feast,
The king at the head, with a greedy eye,
The guests' laughter rings through the room . . .
I will never know.

I will never know what lies beyond,
Be it creatures or kings from long ago
And as I grow old, so does the door
That stands so indifferently upon the oak floor . . .

**Georgia Barden (14)**
**Seaford College, Petworth**

**118**

## Titanic

That maiden voyage will never fade,
After that fine ship was made.
We all marvelled at the boat,
Hoping it would stay afloat.

The finest china had never been used,
While the women were Dawson's muse.
The journey should've taken a month,
But it only travelled just that once.

That night came, just out of the blue,
The rest of this, a surprise to you.
This story took a turn for the worse,
Most lower decks were fit to burst.

Panic struck those unfortunate souls,
All feeling they could hide in holes.
There was not much they could do or say,
To save them from their deaths that day.

The journey didn't last much longer,
We all thought the ship was stronger.
But when it hit that block of ice,
All the passengers scurried like mice.

That maiden voyage will never fade,
After that fine ship was made.
Everyone hoped it would stay afloat,
But it didn't, that poor boat.

**Tilly Gurney (13)**
**Seaford College, Petworth**

## Storm

The land was still and quiet,
A robin, a blue tit sat on a fence
Watching the world go by . . .
But something ahead, they seemed to sense.

It was a cloud, black and low,
In the distance it hovered, forming plans.
The trees, the bushes didn't stand a chance,
Their branches were merely strands!

One bird flew west, one bird flew east
As the monster threw down rain.
Thunder and lightning squabbled,
The trees screamed out in pain!

Trunks were split, leaves were ripped,
The storm cloud then breathed in.
As it breathed in, out came a wind
That turned an oak down,
Down into the din!

But no quicker than it had started,
The black monster turned to grey.
The dying beast spat, the birds flew back,
Back to the bright of day.

**Violet Nicholls (12)**
**Seaford College, Petworth**

## Sayings

How many people are made
Of fingers and thumbs?
Is there sometimes enough blue sky
To make a cat a pair of trousers?
Are you sure you could sew
A silk purse out of a sow's ear?
And you always end up at the doctor's
Even if you do eat an apple a day!

**Phoebe Reid (13)**
**Seaford College, Petworth**

## Summer

You can always tell when it's summer;
The bright green of the grass,
The deep blue of the ocean,
It is almost too hot, but then that light breeze
That tousles your hair cools you down.

After the spring's rain, the sun feels good on your skin,
Kissing your nose and cheeks, leaving them golden.
The roots of your hair get lighter, almost blonde.
Spending all day on the beach with your friends,
Life couldn't get any better.

But then the first summer thunderstorm rolls in,
It is thrilling, frightening and exciting.
Running in the rain on the country club golf course,
Or hearing the pitter-patter on the lakehouse roof,
Looking out over the water and seeing it ripple.

The rest of the year just gets you ready for summer,
Ready for the fun you're going to have.
If there were no summer, it wouldn't be worth it.
Not worth waiting so long for nothing to happen.
I can't wait for that final bell to ring,
To be free.

**Emma Siddall (13)**
**Seaford College, Petworth**

## The Search

They come in the night, every night,
To see if they can find it.
They will never find it.
But they don't know that
Because of who they are.

It is hiding so well that
Nobody would find it,
And definitely not the things
That spend most of their time
Searching high and low for it.

They will never find it,
As they look in the same place all the time,
Just looking and looking and looking,
They don't do anything else
And in the end they waste their lives.

The things they are looking for,
Are their own souls
Lost for thousands of years.
The only place they need to look
Is the only place they will never look.

**Ian Duff (14)**
**Seaford College, Petworth**

## Fire

Fire is a thing, a being, that is feared.
It tortures and eats, such uncontrollable force.

Fire is a beast, wild, fierce and savage.
Can't be tamed nor ever caged, has itself a mind.

Fire is a command, a word pronounced with order.
A word that rages war in depth and heavy mass murder.

Fire is an eternal light, never to cease existence.
Its radiant heat and tender warmth, its only foe to be water.

**Daniel Atkinson (13)**
**Seaford College, Petworth**

**122**

## Confusion

He is
As quiet as nightfall,
As sudden as snow,
Creeping and crawling,
Hiding from sight,
Feeding on doubts.

He loves
Jumping like waves,
Hunting like wolves,
Rushing into battle.
Death is not a problem.
As never-ending as time,
Ever learning,
Ever growing.

He knows
No boundaries,
Never passing.
Ruthless and cruel.
Enemy of knowledge,
Lover of regret.

**Chloe Gooding (13)**
**Seaford College, Petworth**

# Memory

Her tired eyes, they stare into your mind,
You never know what secrets she may find.
Her lovely face, it glows like a light,
Piercing the rich darkness of the night.
Over her shoulders falls her silver hair,
To which the bright moonlight it can compare.
Her body, it stands tall facing the sea,
Remembering the place she had to flee . . .

Up to her house the marching soldiers came,
Carrying her mother so limp and lame.
'Remember me,' her helpless mother cried,
Then in the soldiers' arms, her mother died.
So now she travels back through her own mind,
Back to a place so beautifully divine.
For that is the place she so longs to be,
Where her mind is in perfect harmony.
Words in her head never to be spoken,
Perfect silence never to be broken.

**Ellie Hitchcock (11)**
**Seaford College, Petworth**

# Fear

There lies Fear in the darkest pit of Hell,
Full of hatred are his piercing red eyes;
A soul is taken when Fear rings his bell,
And into death falls a life full of lies.

And when it's night in the graveyard he roams,
The ground shakes as the undead are woken,
In the depths of the night sound deadly groans,
Then you realise that Fear has spoken.

And it is writ in the ancient scroll,
That Fear will eventually steal your soul.

**Archie Reid (11)**
**Seaford College, Petworth**

## Lifeless

I'm sitting here again
Day in, day out
Crippled, can't walk, can't move

I sit in my wheelchair
Watching the children play
Until nightfall when they get ushered in

Then the women come out
And they look at me odd
As if I have no soul, as if I'm dead

I get moved inside at noon
Where I rest for the evening
For the next day I'll repeat it again

I wake up at the break of dawn
To find myself alone for the first time
And yet still, I can't walk, move, I'm nothing.

**Josh Bailey (14)**
**Seaford College, Petworth**


## Sunrise, Sunset

When the sun goes down it's a beautiful sight,
Probably a million people watching its light.
But once it's gone darkness rushes in,
Everyone retreats inside for the fear within.

As the sun has gone and the moon takes over,
People are in bed having dreams of four-leafed clovers.
But for those left out and about in the dark,
Terror consumes them as the evil will embark.

But just as all hope seems lost,
The bringer of light opens with no cost.
Dozy heads and hungover headaches awake,
Not pondering on how long till darkness will wake.

**Charlie Sellers (14)**
**Seaford College, Petworth**

**125**

## Summer Feel

Waking up to a birdsong hymn,
So peaceful as to hear the breeze,
Open the curtains and the sun bursts through,
And pierces my body like the spear of a god,
And draws me in.

So warm, no cold can claim me,
Still so calm is all life around,
The whispering breeze cools the sun,
And floating buds and seed spin by,
And rest on me.

The splashing of water, the laugh of children,
Brings peace to gardens around,
The scent of freshly cut grass and barbecues,
But time flies by and the sun goes down,
Only to wait for another day.

**Calum Syrett (14)**
**Seaford College, Petworth**

## Eternity

She was beautiful.
Girls sighed in her presence,
Boys were left startled.
Everyone was left momentarily blind,
By her one gaze.

She stepped forward,
Her multi-toned hair bouncing,
Her slender figure standing out.
Elegantly.
Impressively.
Her beauty radiating.

Her golden gown flowed behind,
Glittering like raindrops under the light.
She stretched her hand out,
He clasped it firmly.

His jet-black, spiral curls
Touched his shoulder,
His perfect face lit with joy.

I stood,
Watching.

She meant the world to him,
But he was my universe.
He loved her,
I worshipped him.
He would die for her,
I had abandoned myself for him.

I meant nothing to him,
But every cell in my body
Knew of his existence.
I would love him,
For eternity.

**Malika Sachdeva (15)**
**Swakeleys School, Uxbridge**

## Broken Dreams

The glistening eyes dreaming of the future,
Standing in front of the mirror with a tremendous smile.
Tomorrow is the day when I shall be raised from my feet,
When the clouds will dance and the birds will sing.

Yes, that's Jane Eyre from yesterday,
Who dreamed of joy and whose excitement ran through her veins.
Today came an earthquake and shook everything away,
And there lay my broken dreams all shattered in pieces.

A Christmas frost had come at midsummer,
A white December storm had whirled over June.
Ice glazed the ripe apples,
Drifts crushed the blowing roses.

The sorrow in my chest prevented my sleeping,
A restless night and a painful weeping.
A chilly wind begins to blow,
A flame of fire has started to burn my soul.

'Be not far from me, for trouble is near, there is none to help'
Are the only words that uttered from my lips
The gloomy eyes are covering slowly,
My mind is taking me to a better place.

O master, O master of this soul!
The feelings you gave me are shivering in my heart,
Like a suffering child in a cold cradle,
Like a lost bird flying in the freezing wind.

**Sidra Mahmood (17)**
**Swakeleys School, Uxbridge**

## God-Like Being

Wanting to meet God
For something selfish,
Question Him to exist,
Pray for Him, the being in the mist

Why look above for a god,
When they live close to your heart?
They may not seem important, hidden from your eyes,
It's because they blend in with the other's deceit, lies

Help us, without showing it
They teach us, without knowing any better,
And when you really need it, a god is there for you
By your heart and side, and without a clue

You may have met one, loved them so,
Love you back, but how can they be allowed,
So they beautifully crush your chest, where your heart used to be,
No memory or beats left of that celestial glee,

Poor gods, to live for only you,
My dear human, you don't care, seems you never did.
Why they waste their time on apes, is what makes them heavenly
blessed.

**Ross Kennedy (17)**
**Swakeleys School, Uxbridge**

## How Rapid Was That Bird?

How rapid was that bird
Entwining through the trees?
How rapid was that bird
Skimming past the bees?
How rapid was that bird
Evading all the slow ones?
How rapid was that bird?
Not rapid enough to outfly them.

**Callum Reed (11)**
**The Axe Valley Community College, Axminster**

**129**

## Never Again

Sluicing droplets from my bloodshot eyes drench my cheeks,
Eternal entrapment continues to suffocate my already breathless lungs.
My heart enclosed,
Pounding,
Screeching,
Never again will I release it from its darkened skeletal cage.

Feeling merriment and bliss are now forsaken, driven away they are my brighter past.
I am now exiled to a darker life,
Dismal.
Bleak.
Never again will I awake the slumbering memories that veil my past for fear of splintering my artificial reality.

Taking a moment, I glance down at her vacant features that will forever be engraved inside my mind.
Her eyes, once tranquil, I notice now are
Blank.
Glazed.
Never again will I see them sparkle like when her heavenly gaze met mine.

Caressing timidly at her silky, perfect lips I imagine them form that radiant smile.
The smile that once filled my days with
Energy.
Light.
Never again will I see the thing that enlightened my pitiful existence.

Running my rough fingers through her flawless auburn hair.
The pearly aurora,
Illuminating.
Igniting.
Never again will I see that fiery glimmer, both the midday moon and midnight sun inflict upon it.

Elapsing moments glide along, ignorant to the present events.
Silence looms quickly entwining around my embrace,
Chilling.

Intimidating.
Never again will I experience the luxury of a happy sound.

Weeping in the cloudy heavens, a thousand angels.
Their silent tears crystal-blue,
Cascade.
Descend.
Never again will I let them conceal the love I felt for her for now they
swamp me with sorrow and anguish.

**Megan Weaver (14)**
**The Axe Valley Community College, Axminster**


## Young Generation

What are they coming to, the young generation?
We used to be such a lovely nation.
Drugs and alcohol have blown their minds,
Kids abandon their childhood and leave it behind.
They grow up too soon and before we know,
They're lying in a ditch in the slime below.
Going down to the park and smoking some rollies,
Before they know it, their mind's doing roly-polys.
Hanging out on the streets till the early morn,
Then going home to sleep at the crack of dawn.
Getting involved in crime and abuse,
Then running from the cops trying to get loose.
Too hard to admit to being afraid,
Being respected and praised is what they crave.
They skive off school and bunk off work,
All they do is roam around and lurk.
They will never earn a proper wage,
Because all they do is pick on people half their age.
When they grow up they will realise,
'Being hard is cool' was a load of lies.
They did not know it was not allowed,
All they were doing was following the crowd.
So bring up your children and tell them to say,
No to drugs, crime and alcohol and to live life the correct way.

**Matilda Board (14)**
**The Axe Valley Community College, Axminster**

**131**

## Pacific

All of us seasick
Fatigued before we start
Some of us make jokes
Trying to be light-hearted
We know that familiar sound
One we've grown to fear
We don't see it
The thing we can hear
Then it's above us
Red spot on each wing
The door opens
We know what that will bring
*Bang!* One man's down
As we storm the beach
I see the gun muzzle flashes
The captain shouts, 'It's the beach hut we must reach'
That's when I see the man
Clasping his chest
I'll help him if I can
I kneel next to him
I hear a cry
I look up the beach
And that's when some man shouts, 'Banzi'
His sword, his flesh
I bleed like a stream
I fall to the ground
Red it gleams
Just before I black out
I see two men
They have a stretcher
I smile at them
And I close my eyes
And dream of the good old days.

**Charlie Helbert (12)**
**The Axe Valley Community College, Axminster**

## Drink Driving

I knew I should have stopped at one
But the drink was so addictive
And once the craving had begun
I suddenly was evicted

The barman said I'd had enough
Then my belly rumbled
If only he didn't act so tough
Then on the floor I tumbled

I stumbled outside the bar
And puked all on the ground
Then made my way into my car
Car keys are what I found

I started it up and then pulled out
It was getting hard to see
I was having fun without a doubt
But what's come over me?

I'm getting uncontrollably tired
Bright lights are just ahead
My breaking plan just backfired
Soon I will be dead.

My ribs are ripping out my chest
My breathing is getting slower
It's all my fault I must confess
My voice is getting lower

It's now impossible to breathe
I think I'm going to die
All of a sudden I feel relieved
As in my car I lie.

**Leanne Ives (13)**
**The Axe Valley Community College, Axminster**

133

# Heroes In Rags!

Brightly coloured sweets displayed in the window
Xboxes, touch phones and iPod nanos
These are the things that some kids don't get
But others do with a nod of their head.
Some kids would die for a pair of shoes
A mother to hold on to when they caught the flu
Christmas time especially, when families reunite
Coming down from LA just for that one night.
It's sad to see little kids with everything they want
They take many things for granted
Not realising how much they've got!
Kids with an education don't ever wish to learn
But in other places, anywhere, for a child that's all they yearn.
There are families who live in private drives
Who know all the celebs and footballer wives
But then, there are others out there in need of some help
They're homeless and ill, with no strength to yelp.
Every day, twice a day, they walk to a pump
Where they fetch water on their head in a lump
Imagine eating rice every single day
No crisps, no curry, no crème brulée!
They live in shacks, no larger than a shed
Maybe a blanket and the floor for a bed
Little kids surviving on their own
Their parents have died, they've nowhere to go.
Whilst most kids enjoy themselves with their friends
There are some who don't
For they work to pay family mends
Times are hard when there's no food
But they carry on like any hero would!

**Lucie Searle (14)**
**The Axe Valley Community College, Axminster**

134

## Riverbank Bird

Sitting on branch, hidden among the fluttering leaves,
A feathery dart racing down at 25 miles per hour to hit his target.
Swift, fast, clean,
His eyes fixed on the prize.
Shooting down as if from a rifle.
A spiritual spear heading for the portal.
He's in!
As his prey tries to quickly swerve away,
Two feet down, his sequinned eye on the fish,
His feathers wet, his heart beating faster.
The only proof that the blaze of blue has hit the water,
Is a ruffling ripple on the surface.
Little do the humans know, the action going on below.
His scaly supper flicking her transparent tail.
Too late!
The fish is out of his depth, so he swims up into the open.
The droplets of water fall from his wings
As he looks up over the water.
Quick, the kingfisher sees another shoal.
As if he is lightning,
He bolts down and plunges into the river.
This way, that way, which one shall I pick?
Finally, he opens his beak and the silvery fish slips in.
With victory at last, the bird flies up,
Up, up to his territory, among the branches.
A short, sharp slap to ensure his tasty treat will be his to eat,
So he swallows it whole as he looks across the river.
He is indeed a king of fishers,
As proud as a kingfisher can be.

**Misti Lekimenju (12)**
**The Axe Valley Community College, Axminster**

135

# Do You?

Do you miss me?
I miss you.
Have you ever missed anyone
The way I miss you?

Do you want me?
I want you.
Have you ever want anyone
The way I wanted you?

Do you need me?
I need you.
Have you ever need anyone
The way I needed you?

Do you love me?
I love you.
Have you ever loved anyone
The way I love you?

I miss your kiss,
I want your romance,
I need your lead,
I love your company,
The one question I ask
And I ask you to answer it true,
Do you really want all of this too?

**Chloe Yates (14)**
**The Axe Valley Community College, Axminster**

136

## Summer

When the summer's here,
Everyone laughs and cheers,
Some people go abroad,
On expensive holidays others can't afford.

The nice hot sun,
Helps everybody have fun,
Little kids play with beach balls,
But then their parents call.

There's always some snob,
Who's happy to dob,
Your fun little game
As a big, annoying pain.

Wearing big sunglasses,
And trying to swim the fastest,
Eating lots of ice cream
And running until you scream.

Making the biggest sandcastle
And trying not to cause hassle,
Lying there catching a tan
And hitting flies by your Coke can.

This is what summer's all about,
Sun, sea and sand without a doubt.

**Caitlin King (14)**
**The Axe Valley Community College, Axminster**

## My Life At School

Walking . . .
Walking through the corridor

Laughing . . .
Laughing at me and my bag

Staring . . .
Staring at me with eyes like daggers

Pointing . . .
Pointing at the lonely geek, me

Tears . . .
Tears running down my face

Shoving . . .
Shoving past me without a care

Reading . . .
Reading my thoughts, they know I'm scared

Kicking . . .
Kicking my lunch box down the hall

Finding . . .
Finding new ways to torment me

Bullies . . .
Need I say more?

**Milly Chaplyn (12)**
**The Axe Valley Community College, Axminster**

## The Hickley Gammber Wolf

'Twas a beautiful day in the Springle woods
The tintum sun shining bright
A carefree boy walked down Nikkely Path
In the raggedy edge of town Gween

Turn, cross, turn around
Went the thoughtless boy
In search of the one, the only one
The Hickley Gammber wolf

Its bark will shake the birds from the trees
Its teeth will shed your skin
Its breath will quickly captivate you
Its hunger taking over fast . . .

Into the Springle woods he went
10 wingle arrows at hand
And there was the very same
The Hickley Gammber wolf

'What happens next?' I hear you cry
Well, no one ever knew
All that was heard that fateful day
Was a lily-wilting scream . . .

**Pippa Groves (11)**
**The Axe Valley Community College, Axminster**


## Summer Dreams

Children playing in the street,
Laughing loud, looking sweet,
The summer romance and that special kiss,
The good times you don't want to miss.
Late night parties for the teens,
Since winter we started these summer dreams,
Warm breeze and sun in the sky,
Do you love summer as much as I?

**Amy Shiner (14)**
**The Axe Valley Community College, Axminster**

139

## I Think My Mum's A Vampire!

I think my mum's a vampire,
I know it sounds insane,
She went out one night
And she's never been the same.

At school people look and laugh,
I didn't see why
Then I realised she should never be the same.

She comes when it's dark,
She never sees the light,
We never use light bulbs, we always use the candle,
When she comes in she's always dying for a bite.

I can't invite my friends round for the night,
Because all they ever get is a massive fright.
They run and scream,
My mum loves to see them squeal.

When my dad heard my theory,
He said, 'That's quite absurd, but I understand,
Allow me to explain, your mum's not a vampire,
She just works the night-time shift.'

**Darius Pickering (12)**
**The Axe Valley Community College, Axminster**


## Family Photos

Get everyone together
And stand them in line.
Don't forget to smile and say cheese.
Someone sets the camera,
But where's the final family member?
Find them and return to your place,
Someone makes a comment or pulls a face.
Everyone turns around or laughs,
Camera takes the photo.
Oh well, it's just another perfect family picture.

**Mel Ayres (13)**
**The Axe Valley Community College, Axminster**

**140**

## Collector's Piece

Roll up, roll up and come and buy
A huge, squished, mashed-up fly.

Who wants a maths test half right?
Oh please Nigel, Alice, don't fight.

Who wants this amazing collector's piece?
The wool pulled from my old fleece.

Now everything is half price
Except for this out of date rice.

How about this old pencil case?
Oh, for goodness sake, it's not a race.

One pound, two pounds, three pounds, four
No, no, don't let anybody else through the door.

Come here Claire, look at this lovely stinky sock
It will match your new nice blue frock.

Oh, we are so dazed
At how much we raised . . .

Oh . . . nothing!

**Heidi Miller (12)**
**The Axe Valley Community College, Axminster**

## Out Of Touch

There he is at the top of the gorge
A sight hard to ignore
On the bike standing poised
His hands shaking he swears, oh boy!

The crowd jeers and shouts, 'You're' dead'
Confidence gone, filled with dread
He psyches himself up
Ready to go

His bike snakes the rear a craze
The tyres soon to be ablaze
He lets go, the brake ceases
He shoots forward, speed increases
Leaving the ramp behind

The engine stops, his heart skips a beat
The fans watch to see if he survives
This feat through the air he flows
A silent angel on the go
He braces
His eyes close . . .

**Thomas Underdown (12)**
**The Axe Valley Community College, Axminster**

142

## He's Always

He's always sweet,
He's always kind,
He's always there in my mind.

He's always loving,
He's always caring,
He's always funny when he's daring.

He's always loyal,
He's always bright,
He's always there to hold me tight.

He's always cool,
He's always calm,
He's always there to try and charm.

He's always breathtaking,
He's always confusing,
He's always the best when amusing.

He's always occupied,
There's never enough time, but . . .
He's always and forever going to be mine.

**Jessica Barrett (14)**
**The Axe Valley Community College, Axminster**

## Depressed Richness

As a young teen,
I had to be seen,
Because I was not smart,
Flying into a wall like a dart,
All I wanted was the money,
So I could buy a bunny,
I couldn't be stopped,
The money never got dropped,
There was a hunch,
That I had saved a bunch,
I could go to bars,
In my ten cars,
But it didn't last long,
I couldn't sing a song,
Suddenly becoming older,
And a lot bolder,
My money flew in,
This time to the bin,
At the age of forty-one,
They got me with their gun.

**Jack Spencer (14)**
**The Axe Valley Community College, Axminster**


## The Guitar

The guitar is all I need
If it breaks then I will bleed
The guitar as bright as the sun
I'd love to see it being played by a nun

The guitar that put me in a band
Then took me on holiday where I lay in the sand
The guitar that made me rich
But then I lost all the money and I live in a ditch

Now I am homeless thanks to the guitar
And now my head's going a little bizarre.

**Thomas Richards (12)**
**The Axe Valley Community College, Axminster**

 **144**

## You Were, Now You're Not

You were my pet,
The kind that was supposed to stay.

I wish I couldn't remember,
That day you ran away.

When you were around,
You gave me love and happiness every day.

We sat and played,
Until the day went away.

That's why my heart broke,
When Mum said you had been and gone.

I looked up and down,
Till the sun set

And the day you left,
Half my heart was broken.

I miss you,
I miss you until the thought went away.

**Mikila Vernon (11)**
**The Axe Valley Community College, Axminster**


## I Am . . .

Terrified,
Scared,
Lonely,
Sad,
Frightened,
Hurt,
Afraid,
Bruised,
A loser,
Conscious, I am . . .

Bullied.

**Ellie Price (12)**
**The Axe Valley Community College, Axminster**

**145**

# Race Cars All Racing

Race
Leader keeping
Up the pace, going to
Win the race

Cars
All
Revving and
Swerving

Accelerate
Left!
Left!

Right!
*Argh!*
Crashing
Into
Iron
Gates.

**James Blockwell (13)**
**The Axe Valley Community College, Axminster**


# How I Feel!

I am strong because I am weak,
I am beautiful because I know my flaws,
I am a lover because I'm a fighter,
I am fearless because I've been afraid,
I am wise because I have been foolish,
And I can laugh because I've known sadness,
But although I know all these things,
I am no different to anyone else,
I'm proud of the way I am and look and so I should be.
Hopefully, one day all this nonsense about being beautiful and popular,
Will fade away and stop interfering with our lives!

**Shannon Barker (12)**
**The Axe Valley Community College, Axminster**

## One Of Them!

I don't want to do it
But I have to do it
I do do it
But I don't like doing it
I know it's wrong but it makes them happy
Hitting like them
Kicking like them
I don't know why
It makes me sick
I only do it to fit in with them
I don't want to do it
But I do do it
I have to do it
I don't want to be one of them
But I am one of them
I am a bully
Just like them
I only wanted a friend, only one.

**Annabelle Manwaring (12)**
**The Axe Valley Community College, Axminster**


## Rain

Thunder, lightning, wind and rain,
This awful weather is completely insane.
No sun, just rain and hail for weeks,
We've been having many water leaks.

I watch it trickle down the windowpane,
Bounce off the ground, then down the drain.
I'm stuck inside with nowhere to go,
The weather forecast was supposed to be snow.

I want to go out and I want to have fun,
Why can't we have just a little bit of sun?
Thunder, lightning, wind and rain,
This awful weather is completely insane!

**Leah Champion (12)**
**The Axe Valley Community College, Axminster**

147

## What's The Point?

Do we actually know what we're fighting for?
If it's not even worth dying for!
What is the actual definition of the word 'war'?
Who cares what it may be, it's just happening more.
Guns and grenades, what's the purpose?
It only ends in death and destruction, it's just pointless.
Families and homes completely destroyed,
After many millions of soldiers and bombs deployed.
There's the RAF, army, navy and marines,
To be honest they're just words to me.
Everyone being sent over to Afghanistan
Where their version of the army is the Taliban.
They'll shoot or bomb anything that moves,
Would the English citizens really approve?
Even still people are recruiting for the forces,
They have all these self-defence courses.
But really they should teach them about human rights,
Then they can decide whether to put up a fight.

**Jade Lynch-White (13)**
**The Axe Valley Community College, Axminster**


## War On Terra

The end of the world
Is a speculated thing
Innocent lives in pain
The whole world burning

Many believe it is nature's grace
Others believe we will end ourselves
They believe there are many reasons for this
Some purely because of the hatred that dwells

However it is
Chemical, biological
Emotional, political
We believe it will happen.

**Jack Munday (13)**
**The Axe Valley Community College, Axminster**

## Stuck For Ideas

Here's a poem but I don't know what to say,
Maybe I could talk about war, dying or pain,
I had to do it or else I would face
A week of detentions and being whacked with a mace.

She said it could rhyme
And had to be done in time.
The others were doing theirs about crime,
One student talked about alien slime.

I wasted the first lesson,
As I was stuck for ideas,
My mind went blank,
I was sure about that.

However, my ideas were rubbish and useless,
So I did a poem all about that.
It went quite well in fact.
I got in the book, I was amazed and gobsmacked!

**Jack Paddick (14)**
**The Axe Valley Community College, Axminster**


## My Bike

I have bought myself a pit bike
I ride it on a specialised site
The site has a light
So I can ride day and night
I ride with my mates
And we all fly over the gates
My mates have different bikes
Spitfire provides their tyres
But my brother provides mine
He has a KTM
But Aaron only has an STM
They don't ride together
They don't even like each other.

**Ash Wilson Briant (12)**
**The Axe Valley Community College, Axminster**

**149**

## There Is A Creature

There is a creature
That fights among strength
That lives with gallantry
That has endless capability.

There is a creature
That is top of their game
That runs amongst others
That has a wild spirit.

There is a creature
That we will do anything for
That we love and care for.

There is a creature
Who cannot be thoroughly portrayed
Whose movements cannot be captured.

The horse.

**Lana Hughes (13)**
**The Axe Valley Community College, Axminster**


## A Summer Day

The sun is so bright
In the morning light
Lots of lovely flowers to see
Full of pollen for a hungry bee
I watch the clouds drifting in the sky
Whilst I'm eating a meat pie
Birds all singing in the trees
Branches swaying in the breeze
Moon so high in the sky
With the stars so nearby
When I go to bed at night
They will no longer be in my sight
When my alarm will ring
What will the next day bring?

**Adele Gage (13)**
**The Axe Valley Community College, Axminster**

## Our Love Will Never End

As I stared into your eyes,
I realised that time had flied,
It's a pity that once we fell out
And I knew that you would no longer be about.

But now I've found you once again,
I knew our love would never end.
Until the day I saw your wife,
And I just wanted to get at her with a knife.

Behind the tears, hatred and anger,
I still feel that we should be together,
I love you
And I know that you love me too,
So let's get back together
And make sure that we will last forever and ever.

**Sophie Windsor (14)**
**The Axe Valley Community College, Axminster**


## Going To Work

I wake up at the crack of dawn
With a big yawn
Car horns beeping
Sheep are bleating
Birds in the trees singing
My alarm is ringing
I get up ready for work
And I look in the mirror and smirk
I am all tidy and neat
Ready to sit in my office seat
The phones are ringing
The coffee lady is singing
My table is full of files
Will I ever get rid of these piles?

**Fiona Gage (13)**
**The Axe Valley Community College, Axminster**

**151**

## True Beauty In You

True beauty is in the way you laugh,
True beauty is in your eyes,
True beauty is how you act,
True beauty is inside,
True beauty is unseen,
True beauty is yourself,
True beauty can't be cruel,
True beauty is bare,
True beauty is within you,
True beauty is always there,
True beauty can't be covered up,
True beauty means true love,
True beauty is the flight of a dove,
True beauty is all that matters after all!

**Emma Sharp (12)**
**The Axe Valley Community College, Axminster**


## My Life

Life is good, and it's bad.
Life is happy, life is sad.
Life is loving and it's hating.
Life is fast-moving, life is waiting.
Life is running and it's walking.
Life is silence, life is endless talking.
Life is a whisper and a shout.
Life is staying in, life is hanging out.
Life is sleeping and it's waking.
Life is knowing, life is anticipating.
Life is my life and my life is you.
I spend my life hoping you'll love me too.

**Emily (Rosie) Clarke (14)**
**The Axe Valley Community College, Axminster**

## Behind The Curtains

I stand behind,
In the shadows
Nobody sees me
Behind the curtain

The crowd waits
Watching the stage
They never look
Behind the curtain

You go out
You act your part
But you never see
That I'm behind the curtain

And you never see
What you mean to me
To you, I'm just a girl
The girl behind the curtain

You rush past
You break my heart
Who ever notices
The girl behind the curtains?

I just want you to know
The truth about my dreams
That I don't want to be
The girl behind the curtain

I'll wait for you to see
Everything I can be
Until then I'm just me
The girl behind the curtain

**Natasha Cross (13)**
**Torquay Girls' Grammar School, Torquay**

# On The Other Side

If death was an animal,
I know what it would be,
A blind little mole,
Coming after me.

None of us would know,
Not me or the mole,
What was to come,
As we entered our hole.

If death was a sound,
I know what it would be,
A rushing waterfall,
Falling continuously.

An item of peace,
Forever in your mind,
A source of comfort,
Never leaving you behind.

If death was a symbol,
I know what it would be,
A bridge over water,
And a leaf from a tree.

A circle would surround it,
To symbolise life before you died,
The bridge as you would cross it,
And the leaf a new side.

**Sophie Coe (14)**
**Torquay Girls' Grammar School, Torquay**

## Untitled

Battles raging, fierce and bloody
Groans escape me,
My friends torn down around me,
My face jagged and cut.
Lashing rain like daggers,
My body hurt and edging to oblivion.
My hair lashing me as the wind howls.

My roots weary from clutching at the earth holding me firm.
Any hope of mercy evaporated by the sheer cruelty of my tormentor,
Nature against me, but as fearless before my agony,
As I am an ancient tree.

In the darkness a child and a tree huddle.

A short distance afar, another faces the wrath of Nature.
Thunder deafening, lightning allowing a reprieve from the darkness.
In the distance a mighty oak stands firm.
Staggering she reaches the safe haven at last.

Darkness clinging like unwanted dirt
Making the tree look daunting and mysterious
But it is a shelter, a hope against pain,
Like a ray of light in a thunderstorm.
The storm seems endless.
When will it stop and lay to rest?

**Anna Seifert-Craggs (13)**
**Treviglas Community College, Newquay**

155

## Her Last Words

I feel like an animal,
A wolf killing my prey
But to me he deserved it
He turned me into this person

My crumbled up home is where
I will leave and here by my side,
Frisky will be
I'm on my way but I've done my worst

I'm happy now,
I will see my son soon
I have lived alone for too long

I'm letting go
I'm going home.

**Emma Tillson (14)**
**Wadham School, Crewkerne**


## Untitled

I stare at a blank canvas,
Thoughts and feelings torturing my brain,
The only way out is pain and misery,
The scent of blood fills the air,
I think to myself, *what would life be like if none of this started?*
*What would life be like without you?*
And then it hits me like a bullet,
I've already lost you,
I'd have nothing to lose,
The presence of death slowly creeping through my veins,
The last strike of excruciating pain is over,
What once was a depressing story has come to an end,
I'm gone.

**Danielle Wakeman (14)**
**Wadham School, Crewkerne**

## Marriage Is Not Bound Under Ground

Lonely, isolated, the village of death town,
Dare no one enter, or consequences shall fall down.
Where the dead souls perished, fear that love cannot be found,
For the deceased and the living, marriage is not bound -
And within that town lay a corpse of a lady,
Who died, a tragic accident by a gunshot sound.

Pale, crisp white was the colour of her skin,
She was buried with a black cotton dress up to her chin.
Her lips were once a cherry red, but now a crimson black,
Her eyes gave a frozen stare, so dark and beady black -
And her devil-red hair remained precisely the same shade,
But if she found her one true love, her life would be a shame.

With a bow-tie on his neck and a dime in his hand,
This young, handsome bridegroom strolled the dim lit land.
Never would he have known that a grave was what he stood on,
For now, something mystifying was sure to cast upon.
Yet the bridegroom was unaware of the place he was in,
His coming wedding was so certainly planned.

So silent, so dark, the bejewelled night sky was like a magical
eclipse.
A cold, slim hand reached out and grabbed the bridegroom's closest
limb.
The earth started to shake and so soon a lady stood before him;
This lady was no ordinary being, for she owned a secret grin.
She said to the bridegroom, 'You are the one.'
But he replied, 'My love for you is so much dim.'

One forward step and a kiss was all it took,
For the bridegroom to fathom the lady's feelings and her sorrowful
look.
She pleaded him to follow her down under,
But lightning struck and made him wonder.
'In no less than a month, the lady in waiting will be my eternal mate.'
So he wiped off her kiss, and took off in a brisk.

**Emily Yuen (13)**
**Wallington High School for Girls, Wallington**

**157**

# The Ballad Of Her Final Pact

The trees closed over the pathway, as the wind blew into the night.
The stars in the sky were like candles, glowing so strong and so
bright.
The rain started to fall on the ground, where the young knight
galloped along.
His steed so handsome, his armour so proud,
His sword hanging powerful and strong.

His eyes were as blue as the ocean, his hair was a ruby-red.
His armour was a strong silver shield, covering his beautiful head.
So as he galloped along the road, his coat hanging off his back.
His steed so handsome, his armour so proud,
And yet only his love did he lack.

He closed his eyes and he pictured her, the bluest of eyes staring
back.
Her beautiful curls were like soft waves, shining the darkest of black.
He could almost hear her voice calling, 'Leave me, please leave me
young knight.'
His steed so handsome, his armour so proud,
He then witnessed the most terrible sight.

His beloved was tied up so strong, to an oak tree standing high.
The leaves whispered sadness and sorrow, until she turned round to
cry.
'Don't come any closer I warn you.' He ignored her wise alert.
His steed so handsome, his armour so proud,
As he rode to her through the dirt.

He leapt off his horse and went over to untie from the hold.
He stood up tall with a glint in his eye, his knife in his hand, looking
bold.
A gunshot startled the atmosphere, and the blood poured through his
hand.
His steed so handsome, his armour so proud,
As he fell to his knees on the land.

A silhouette appeared from the darkness, with malice and hate in his
eyes.
'Take me I pray thee let my love go,' with a desperate plea to the
skies
So as the shot sounded he'd left her, she then vowed to make her
final pact.
His steed so handsome, his armour so proud,
No longer true love did he lack.

**Annabelle Smith (13)**
**Wallington High School for Girls, Wallington**

## The Leviathan

Rise up before me,
Bluestone colossus, out of the Atlantic.
A fistful of God and an eyeful of terror
The rough-hewn face of a tyrant.

Leviathan king, titanic Adonis.
The Kraken and the Hydra and Cthulhu in your thrall,
The leaden sea in your grasp.
Call up the creatures of the abyss.

Iron-clad white horses break at your thighs.
With his cry, who is like God?
Freakish behemoth, your ancient city in ruins at your feet
Summon Atlantis.

Rise up, Goliath, from the deep.
Crash the surface and breech the sky.
Bring forth the tempest, the raging flood;
Your torrential kingdom Atlantis.

**Heather Bennett (14)**
**Wallington High School for Girls, Wallington**

# The Ballad Of William's Love

A young boy called William had worked in a mine,
He liked a fair maiden, her name was Lilly and she was so divine.
He always woke up bright and early, for he was out of sight,
He spoke, 'I want her to be my all, I am willing to fight.'

Lilly was a tall girl, attractive, pretty and rich,
Whenever William would just stop and stare, he would always twitch.
She was known for her luscious lips and beautiful hips,
Her hair glowed like the stars, and she wore freshly picked flowery clips.

William was a short lad who lived in the grubby slums,
Every time he ate, he would drop lots of crumbs.
His hair was awfully messy and he was passionate to drink wine,
As soon as he saw Lilly, a nervous chill ran up his spine.

As they grew old, William was too afraid to speak,
He got butterflies in his stomach and felt extremely weak.
One day he thought, 'I have to go tell her how I feel.'
He was in his own little bubble, a dream which felt surreal.

William had watch'd the small droplets of water trails roll down the glass the next day,
He couldn't believe his eyes on what he saw, from this day on he was in dismay.
He heard the wind tugging and bashing against the trees with anger and rage,
There was little Lilly with her man who had looked a lot older of his age.

Lilly and her boyfriend were so crazily in love,
They were like two peas in a pod, almost like a beautiful white dove.
They were both skipping, skipping, skipping all day long.
They spent every minute together always singing a song.

Weeping William had left a note on his bedroom door,
There William was who had committed suicide, lying dead pale on
the floor.
It said, 'I did not achieve to win my love and therefore I will never
succeed.'
His heart was broken, and his soul had disappeared indeed.

**Aysha Uddin (13)**
**Wallington High School for Girls, Wallington**

# Hate

He fills you up inside until he poisons your veins,
He empties out your mind, but only one thing remains.
He shoves the pain of aggression and bitterness towards you,
And out comes emotion in which you thought you never knew.
With subtle little cracks that begin to appear,
Running around desperately, he's feeding on fear.
Like a python, he's entrancing, waiting to make his next move,
Digging into your thoughts like a shovel making its groove.
A fierce incision, carving his territory where he'll haunt again,
Leaving ruins and wrecks of once noble men.
Direct or indirect he will possess you,
He's just a phase that no one can get through.
He will always have presence within you; he will never be overcome,
He will work all through day and night just to turn your heart numb.

**Ashleigh Wherry (13)**
**Wallington High School for Girls, Wallington**

# The Ballad Of The Shaking Of Haiti

It was an afternoon in January,
Just like any other day,
The innocent locals were joyous and merry,
Working at the beach, under the sun's hot ray,
But that was before the ground shook poor Haiti.

Beyond shimmering sand, a town filled with love,
A safe refuge for many,
The folk as happy as the sun shining above,
The greatest atmosphere as true as any,
But that was before the ground shook poor Haiti.

Port-au-Prince school children were thought to be safe,
But who could have really helped?
The teachers cried, 'Do not panic, you must have faith!'
But the children lost hope, they screamed and they yelped,
The ground had just begun to shake poor Haiti.

The buildings collapsed, an avalanche of brick,
Volatile Earth was waking,
Aroused from its slumber, the scene was chaotic,
The ground was a shaking, shaking, shaking,
The ground it was shaking, Lord, help Haiti.

Crash! The towns caved in -
Shrieks, trapping them inside,
Crushing kind souls, friend and foe;
Their beloved homes were burying them alive;
Never had they known so much pain and sorrow;
Oh please make it stop.
The ground shook poor Haiti.

Homes gone, families lost, bodies in the streets,
Some devoured by the Earth,
Or smothered and broken by the falling concrete,
Killed brutally as if nothing they were worth,
The shaking stopped, now the suffering begins.

**Mikayla Sinclair (13)**
**Wallington High School for Girls, Wallington**

**162**

## The Ballad Of The Wrong Marriage

The sun was out, the sky bright blue, a tear ran down her face,
Her long white dress blew in the wind, it was pretty and lined with
lace.
She picked a flower off a bush and placed it in her hair,
She was the prettiest in all the land, she was dainty and fair.

She had long wavy hair, brown like her father's used to be,
She had lips like cherries, and out of pale green eyes did she see.
She was smart like her mum used to be, but she died last year,
She tried to stop crying but she couldn't, so out came tear then tear.

Her dad looked round to see his daughter, 'Oh you look so nice!'
'Dad this is wrong, this is all wrong! I hate him! It's him I despise.'
'Nonsense my dear, he's the one for you, a dad knows these things.'
'Really Father? I doubt it, and I refuse to put on that ring.'

She tried to walk quickly away, but her dad took her arm,
He said, 'If you marry him, there'll be no harm.'
She thought to herself, *why is my dad so mean?*
Then she realised, *he wants his money, it seems.*

She picked up her diary that was on her bedside desk,
I do not love him, she wrote. He is horrid, he's mean and grotesque,
Who cares if he's rich? I don't! He won't be the one I wed,
My love will arrive, he said he would come, my one true love, Wilfred.

The wedding song played whilst her father was linked to her arm,
She was so pleased, she knew her love would come and cause that
beast some harm.
The priest asked the beast, 'Do you take this woman?'
'Yes I do.'
She shed a tear because he wasn't coming and that much she knew.

She had to say yes, because she was too nice to say no,
She cried herself to sleep most nights because he didn't show.
Can you now see why she cried that day in her wedding dress?
Because Wilfred never showed up, she was forced to say, 'I do, yes.'

**Sophie Garrod (12)**
**Wallington High School for Girls, Wallington**

163

# The Ballad Of The Secret Love

Sitting in front of the TV all alone,
Her parents had left her, they were not at home,
Sophie waited for her sweetheart to appear,
She hoped he would come soon, she hoped he was near,
She could not tell her parents, she did not dare,
Or she and him would be shot dead then and there.

A tap at the window, a peek through the door,
And Jacob's face was the thing Sophie then saw,
He came in the house and took Sophie's white hand,
Sophie was pretty with hair like golden sand,
He looked in her eyes, 'I missed you,' he told her,
She smiled, content, he was just like no other.

Then Jacob leaned in and kissed her soft, pale lips,
She hesitated, she had never done this,
But Sophie loved him more than anything else,
She leaned in, 'I missed you too,' she then did tell,
'I have waited so long for this sweet moment,'
Jacob whispered, 'please, let's just make it perfect.'

Jacob threaded a necklace round her neck,
She looked at him stunned, she did not then expect,
Shouting, banging, booming voices from outside,
'You said you'd never see him again, you lied!'
Her father's voice, she instantly recognised,
Sophie's dad then came bursting into the room,
'D'you expect me to let him be your groom?'

'Dad, it's not like that!' Sophie pleaded away,
Jacob's face was full of horror and dismay,
Sophie's dad then drew out a silver bullet,
And loaded it into the shiny musket,
'I love you,' they whispered, prepared for their doom,
As they gazed at each other, the gun went boom.

**Megan Steer (13)**
**Wallington High School for Girls, Wallington**

164

## The Ballad Of The Other Love Of Marcus

Gusty wind tugged at the hair of the young man,
He pulled his long, black cloak closer as he ran.
Thunder rumbled and lightning struck a lone tree,
The man pulled off his hood so that he could see.
And people shrank back from the stare of Marcus.

The eyes of Marcus were as blue as could be,
His ugly, scarred face was not pleasant to see.
His long brown hair was scraped in a ponytail,
His black cloak billowed behind him, like a sail.
And people shrank back from the stare of Marcus.

He ran to a woman, 'Hermione come,
You cannot stay out here while there is no sun.'
'I cannot,' she replied, 'You go on alone,
Please look after my child until I get home.'
And people shrank back from the stare of Marcus.

Marcus ran to the house of Hermione,
Told his other love and friends to come party.
Hermione snuck in through the back way,
She stared at the scene with a look of dismay.
And people shrank back from the stare of Marcus.

Hermione said, 'Get out!' She waved a gun,
'Or you and your girlfriend will be dead and gone!'
Everyone scarpered; they headed for the door,
But they were squashed, many landed on the floor.
And they all shrank back from the stare of Marcus.

So Marcus fled and was never seen again,
But his love was not lucky, she was shot dead.
Everyone from the party ran for their lives,
And no one saw Hermione end her life.
Still people shrink back from the stare of Marcus.

**Chani Wray (12)**
**Wallington High School for Girls, Wallington**

# The Ballad Of The Forbidden Love

The silken sea was a bed of diamonds,
The enchanted heavens, as merry as could be,
Where the barmy breeze shook the sweet town St Blair,
Beside the flowing riverbank lay she.
'Hush-hush,' whispered the wind, gliding to the town square.

Alas! The word had spread in the dear town,
That a grand, glorious celebration awaits,
For a local nobleman's daughter must marry.
A fancy beau will no doubt be her fate.
'Hooray, hooray!' the town folk cheer through the alleys.

Yet hidden in the murky gloom wept Bess:
The prosperous but fair young daughter of an Earl.
Rich, dark ebony locks; skin as pale as a dove,
Lips redder than roses, polished like pearls.
'Weep, weep,' cried sweet Bess, 'I'll ne'er be with my true love.'

Her love was nothing but a stable boy,
No wealth, no possessions, poor boy James was his name.
Their love was a fairy tale, built amidst fantasies.
Bess daren't tell her poor Papa - the shame!
*Ding-dong* sang the church bells. Ran out of time was she.

Step by step advanced blessed Bess down the aisle,
And close by stood waiting her feared future, her groom.
Her moist tears ran further than her dazzling dress train,
Weak and helpless, she was sure of her doom.
'I do, I do!' cried ruined Bess through the pain.

Yet every new moon the lovers would meet,
Poor boy James and sweet Bess had one day to be free.
They'd escape beneath the wild cherry tree and pray
For a life as one, how charmed they would be!
Dream, dream . . . they'd be together forever one day.

**Sophie Grant (12)**
**Wallington High School for Girls, Wallington**

166

## Beauty Beneath The Skin

Lonely shadows set upon a deserted purple moor,
A pathway spiralled upwards to an ancient castle door.
The mystic moon shimmered to light the highest tower,
A dragon lay there waiting, casting an evil glower.
Beauty beneath the skin.

The beast with red eyes piercing, scars cut deep in aged scales,
Crouched low against the brick tower, claws sharp as iron-cast nails.
Guarding his fair maiden princess, a prisoner cursed was she,
A prince came riding through the night, his goal to set her free.
Beauty beneath the skin.

The prince had journeyed many a mile, risking life and limb,
Through forest dark and valley deep, under a sky so grim.
Riding upon his mighty steed, white as the driven snow;
A speeding arrow straight and true fired from Cupid's bow.
Beauty beneath the skin.

Courageously he fought the beast, as it roared and tore the air,
He drew his sword, 'For love and honour!' he boldly declared.
The hero cut the dragon down beneath the rising sun.
He ran across the castle yard, a heart he'd surely won.
Beauty beneath the skin.

Rushing up the spiral steps he found the maiden asleep,
She woke and looked up with disdain, her eyes began to weep.
'You are not the prince I dreamed of; handsome and tall was he!'
'But my sweet love,' he replied, 'Then what's to become of me?'
Beauty beneath the skin.

The princess fled in her silk gown, and reached the yard below,
The prince looked down with horror and cried too late, 'Nooooo!'
For the dying dragon lay with the princess, blood round his grin;
The prince sighed, 'Shame she could not see. . . beauty beneath the
skin.'

**Maddie Banthorpe-Peters (13)**
**Wallington High School for Girls, Wallington**

167

# The Ballad Of Lily And Kyle

There once was a young, smart lad called Kyle,
He had the most magnificent smile,
His love for Lily, uncontrollably wild,
'Twas like he had gone back to being a child.
Where was life going for this man, Kyle?

Lily was the fairest in town,
Daughter of the king, heir for the crown,
She also had this undying love for Kyle,
But her father did not allow things so vile,
Was this love story to end so down?

It was a very cool, breezy night,
Lily was going to get a fright,
Kyle climbed up to a place, Lily's balcony,
Lily was scared and not sure what she would see,
Not sure, would it be such a good sight?

Kyle open'd the door and said to Lily,
'Come, let us sail across the vast sea,'
She did so reply, 'Oh, don't be so foolish,'
He answered, 'I'm not! We both know it is our final wish,'
But would Kyle assist his love Lily?

Lily finally gave into Kyle,
Thus too late! They'd been gone for a while,
Kyle took his boat, out to sea they both did sail,
Their love so strong, they would never ever bail,
Would they go on for that extra mile?

On a faraway island they stayed,
On the soft grass they usually lay,
Their love going on did keep them together,
They'd not be apart, going on forever,
Thus a sweet tale of Lily and Kyle!

**Shreena Marsh (13)**
**Wallington High School for Girls, Wallington**

**168**

## The Ballad Of The Broken Tale
## Of The Baker's Boy.

Young Alexander the poor baker's boy,
Really quite handsome and so full of joy.
Yet he was in love with the king's daughter,
But would never be able to court her.

Alexander was a charming young lad,
Who worked at the bakers for his old dad.
He was kind and thoughtful, perfect he seemed
Yet he was poor, apart from in his dreams.

Genevieve was a pretty little thing
And she loved to all day sing, sing, sing, sing!
But secretly she liked Alexander,
Oh, if only he were Alex the Sir.

Sadly there was competition for Gen.
There were too many kind, handsome young men,
But her father preferred evil Khasim.
Whose scary eyes seemed to glitter and gleam.

Alexander knew the king would not sway,
So he thought of a plan to run away.
He crept up to Gen's balcony one night,
And there she stood in a nightgown so white.

He whispered to her, 'Let us leave right now.
We'll escape from here, no one will know how.'
They jumped oh so far, no care of the height
Then escaped quickly, like a flash of light.

They were in the forest, towards the lake,
'Twas cold but they went on for true love's sake.
In the bitter night, they slept near some farms,
And died there frozen in each other's arms.

**Jiamei Goldsmith (13)**
**Wallington High School for Girls, Wallington**

169

# The Ballad Of The Lost Land

A thousand years or more ago,
There was a legend told,
Of a land from which none could return,
However young, strong, or bold.
The few who'd tried had never returned
From the lost land of afar.

Though none had lived to tell the tale
One man was still prepared;
Of the task of finding this lost land,
He was not in the slightest scared.
Vow'd he'd search forever and a day.
For the lost land of afar.

He set off with three simple things;
His steed, broadsword and pride;
He rode, he swam, he scaled cliffs,
He searched for it far and wide.
Till after time, on the horizon,
He saw the lost land of afar.

Ecstatic he galloped until he arrived
At the border where he met the threat -
As tall as the sky with crimson-like blood,
It roared; in stone was his fate set.
He felt fear for the first time on his search
For the lost land of afar.

He was dead before he hit the ground,
The beast had killed him fast,
Alas, like those before him,
His quest was not to last.
The few who've tried have never returned
From the lost land of afar.

**Francesca Morris (13)**
**Wallington High School for Girls, Wallington**

## The Ballad Of Jemma The Jew

There was a woman, who was on her own,
She was stuck in a room, scared and alone,
Her name was Jemma and she was a Jew,
She had been frightened for a year or two,
Cold as ice is what she felt in the room,
Hearing loud noises going, *boom! Boom! Boom!*

She peeked out the window, just a small look,
Turned away quickly, a second that took,
Jemma thought someone saw her, she hoped not,
She heard a loud noise and a knife she got,
Hid behind a door ready to stab him,
Turned to look but completely adored him.

As fit as he was, she could not resist,
She tried to step back and loosen her fist,
He took a step and moved closer,
Their lips met while they moved to the sofa,
'My name's Jai,' he said 'Mine's Jemma,' she said,
She grabbed his hand and pulled him to her bed.

She thought to herself as the time just flew,
*'You are a German and I am a Jew,'*
She said quietly, 'But this is not right,'
'We love each other it's love at first sight,
We're sure to stay together forever,'
Jai said looking lovingly at Jemma.

Three years went and the war kept on going,
Yet Jai and Jemma's love was still flowing,
Until the day a bomb hit Jemma's flat,
It happened so fast; it was just like that,
Jai and Jemma said three words in a mime,
They lay as one for the very last time.

**Priya Wadher (13)**
**Wallington High School for Girls, Wallington**

**171**

## The Ballad Of Sir Alan

Sir Alan always lived in his own little world
Always broke the hearts of poor young girls
Until he met the fair Emaleena
A new side to him was shown when he went to meet her
And then soon, in love he fell
Sir Alan's tale I'm about to tell.

They met in a country barn just outside of town
Their eyes just met and he removed her frown
They danced all night, locked in each other's arms
Both of them completely fallen for each other's charms
He then looked at her and sighed
Little did she know, it was all lies.

He complimented her, said her eyes glowed like stars
And read her the story of Lochinvar
She was happy, but he wasn't the same
Emaleena was loved up, he was playing a game
When the truth was all spilled out
The girl felt betrayed and full of doubt.

Every single thing was wrong, nothing was right
One word would bring tears, he ruined her life
But one sunny day the crying ended
Emaleena realised she was fine, her heart mended
She knew time was all it took
Bad lies and pretence, her whole world shook.

Sir Alan, Sir Alan, what shall we do with you?
You disguised yourself, faces you have two
We know Emaleena deserved much more
Than to be hurt, broken, hopeless and torn
No one knows Alan like me
For Emaleena is I, can't you see?

**Charlotte Griffiths (13)**
**Wallington High School for Girls, Wallington**

## The Ballad Of The Clan Maiden

As the black veil up above hung down,
The glooms of the night glanced upon the town;
The fair maiden of the royal clan,
Rose sat by her bedside crying in her hands;
For the vicious noble she was to wed,
Was not the one that, 'I do' should be said.

She had the beauty of a goddess,
The fair green eyes of morning cress;
Her tender rose lips the colour of early dawn,
Her flowing hair many shades of a young fawn;
Robed in her billowing, rich, golden dress,
All she wanted was to love her man, even after eternal rest.

In a village not too far away,
Lived a young farmer surrounded by hay.
Bold and brave he was sure to be,
John was he called, known to all in Naseby;
If only he wasn't in the peasants clan,
Would his and Rose's dream be a successful plan.

It was the morning of all Rose's dismay,
'Hurry child, the wedding has got to be on its way,'
But all the voices were just a dismal fog,
For she had no reason to marry this fowl dog;
'I'm on my way,' she bravely said,
And without another whisper, she fled.

It was a shame that the bridegroom had to see,
Rose and John were already at the nearby sea;
'John, I'm so glad faith has brought us together,'
'Rose, you are like the water for the sea, we will be forever,'
One gunshot it took through young John to break his promise,
For all she saw was her life at her feet, in utter grimace.

**Tanuja Thavarajah (13)**
**Wallington High School for Girls, Wallington**

# The Ballad Of Cursed Love

Long, long ago on a cold winter's night
Two lovers danced beneath stars that were bright;
Bright as the ring that glinted and shone
In the man's pocket, for the girl he'd won.
He planned to propose, but now wasn't right;
He'd wait till he saw her tomorrow night.

But they did not know, a witch lay in wait
To curse fair Rose as she passed through her gate.
So jealous was she of this girl's lover
She'd do anything for the man to love her.
Now the girl could not look anyone in the eye;
The witch made sure that the person would die.

Her father locked Rose up in a tower,
And the time ticked by hour by hour.
Waiting, waiting ten long years to be free;
Her lover waited too, so faithful was he.
'We'll marry someday,' he told her so sure
That things would work out, happy for evermore.

Meanwhile Rose sat, her green eyes far away,
Mourning time she had lost, three years and a day.
Her long, wavy, black hair flowed down her back;
Dark as night, for beauty she did not lack.
Her skin was pale, her cheeks as pink as the dawn,
But now her features were tired and drawn.

One day from her window, she heard bells ring;
A figure in white, a joyful wedding.
Aghast, she saw that the witch was the bride,
And the man Rose loved was there at her side.
Her heart breaking, she met the witch's eyes;
But the groom was in the way, it was he who died.

**Emily Garbutt (13)**
**Wallington High School for Girls, Wallington**

**174**

## The Ballad Of Jack And Corelina

Sir Jack from Lower Canterbury, a blacksmith was he
He loved dear Corelina and so did she
Every day he drove past in his yellow bubble car
Until he saw the light of the first bright star
They decided that tonight was the night they would meet
Promising themselves that they would only greet not cheat.

They were fixed yet locked at each other's eyes
Unable to move, this was no surprise
Corelina was in love with Sir Jack
So they spent the night locked in the black shack
The next day they awoke in each other's arms
There was no doubt she had fallen for Jack's charms.

Little did she know, he wasn't what he said to be
As he was a liar, a cheat, all for a small fee
He would make them fall in love with him
Then dump them, leaving her feeling dim
But jack had twisted the story around this time
He loved her for real and wouldn't obey the crime.

He could no longer do this to her anymore
He had to leave straight away out of the shack door
She cried after him to never leave and come back
But he needed to pursue his plan of attack
For he would visit his violent boss that night
To quit his horrible job with all his might.

His boss and he argued about the girl till dawn
They then realised this was the end, and were torn
Jack loved her but had betrayed the trust of his boss
The past haunted him that night, the love he had lost
He couldn't take it any longer, a corpse was he
Hurtful Sir Jack, time of death, eleven forty-three.

**Laura Blackmore (13)**
**Wallington High School for Girls, Wallington**

**175**

# The Ballad Of Mel And Michael

Mel and Michael have been friends since forever,
Never apart, always together,
Since nursery they've been like brother and sister,
One day she moved away, he really missed her,
He felt so alone with nobody there,
Now on his lonesome, no one there to care.

When he was at the park he swung on the swings,
Hoping his mobile would ring, ring,
He missed Mel so much he wished she would come home,
He didn't like feeling so down and alone,
He then got a text from Mel that made him smile,
It said, 'Meet me in Starbucks in a small while.'

He met her in Starbucks the very next day,
He asked her, 'Are you here to stay?'
Mel replied with a yes and a big, cheesy grin,
She wished she had never gone to begin.
They were reunited like never apart,
Together forever, friends since the start.

They met up the next week and went for a walk,
Hand in hand, they talked and they talked.
They talked about how they had grown up so much,
And that they wished they could have kept in touch.
But whilst both of them where stuck in the moment,
It started to rain, they had to run forward.

But whilst they were running, Michael didn't look,
Smashed by a car, to hospital was took.
Mel was so scared whether Michael was okay,
She waited and waited, prayed and prayed,
Mel walked away with a tear in her eye,
Michael hadn't made it, that night he had died.

**Hannah Boon (13)**
**Wallington High School for Girls, Wallington**

## The Ballad Of Wrecked Love

She stared impatiently out of the window,
The reason for his lateness; she did not know.
Almost an hour she had been waiting for
She thought to herself, 'Oh, he loves me no more!'
Finally, there came a loud knock at the door
She glanced at the clock and it read half-past four.

She quickly jumped up and fiddled with her hair,
He'd almost stood her up but she didn't care.
Although, she did wonder why he was so late,
She wanted to ask him but she thought she'd wait.
Suddenly a great thought struck her, she froze
*Tonight,* she thought, *he is going to propose!*

She opened the door, forced a smile on her face,
Expected the same, a grin or embrace
But no, his face was as still as a statue
And he said, 'There's something I have to tell you.'
He took her hand and led her to the hallway
Trying to ignore her face with dismay.

She tried to block out the voices in her head
He loved her no more, though it hadn't been said,
'I am very sorry to do this to you,
I am in love with someone else, that is the truth'
After that, they sat in silence for a while
He then got to his feet and gave her a sad smile.

She tried to forget 'bout all the words he had said
It wasn't working; they were stuck in her head.
Suddenly she realised what she had to do,
This was going to be the right thing she knew
She got to the kitchen and pulled out a knife
Tonight was the night she was to end her life.

**Anisha Ahmedabadi (12)**
**Wallington High School for Girls, Wallington**

# The Ballad Of The Begging Girl

The sun was low in the summer sky
The breeze bustling in the trees
Upon a hill in Camelot high
A girl was begging on her knees

She had blonde hair right down to the floor
Her eyes were as blue as the sea
She begged until she could beg no more
For so deeply in love was she

'I hate him!' shouted her father dear
'You must see him no more,
If I see you with him around here,
He will be sorry to the core!'

She ran fast up to her lover's house
To tell him what had happened
Her father followed quiet as a mouse
And saw them, his anger sharpened

'Aha I have seen you together!'
'Ha ha I can kill you now!'
'I have reached the end of my tether'
'I'll kill you by any means how.'

She told him to run to the highlands
Her father would come tonight
He took refuge on a small island
For he did not want a big fight

She ran fast right up to his bedroom
And pulled up the covers tight
A bang broke the silence in the room
And she died for her love that night.

**Ellie Clarke (13)**
**Wallington High School for Girls, Wallington**

## The Ballad of The Lovers' War

Sir Lloyd and Saharah were forced into marriage,
They entered their wedding in a big white carriage,
However Saharah did not feel so complete,
As Sir Lloyd was not the man she wanted to meet.

Sir Lloyd was tall, fair, handsome and a charming man,
With sparkling eyes just like a big blue fan,
But Saharah fell in love with another man,
And Sir Lloyd came up with an evil plan.

Sir Virgil was the man who took Saharah's heart,
He did split Saharah and Sir Lloyd far apart,
They snuck out at midnight and ran far, far away,
Together, hand in hand, forever and a day.

Little did Sir Virgil know, he was onto the pair,
Sir Lloyd then jumped onto his horse in such despair,
The horse galloped along in the cold and wet rain.
With a gun in Sir Lloyd's hand to cause them such pain.

Under the shining stars the couple did make love,
For there was no one in sight except the little white dove,
They stopped as Sir Virgil said to her, 'I love you,'
Saharah was happy and replied back, 'I love you too.'

A loud bang occurred as Sir Lloyd fired the gun,
Supposed to kill he before the couple could run,
Instead Saharah was bleeding a pool of blood,
As Sir Lloyd, shocked, dropped to the ground with a loud thud.

Sir Virgil sat near her stroking her hair crying,
He pecked her on the head as she lay there dying,
He could not live another long day without she,
Picked up her gun and shot it at his head did he.

**Alissa Liu (12)**
**Wallington High School for Girls, Wallington**

# The Ballad Of The Fatal Wedding

As she lifted the veil over her piercing eyes,
She scrutinised this man from her aloof disguise,
The man she would soon accept to be her bridegroom,
Under the watchful eyes of the awaiting room.

The most simple question was spoken, bold and clear,
By the vicar who certainly wanted to hear.
'Yes, yes of course I love thee, O truly I do,
My only wish is to spend my whole life with you!'

But this fair maiden looked anything but certain,
Wishing her golden hair was thick as a curtain,
Her eyes were as blue as the clear sky above,
Tears sprung to her eyes as she thought of her lost love.

The perfect man she met a few summers ago,
But he left her weeping in a calm spring meadow,
With an almighty crash the doors were flung wide,
And the groom had to watch as the man embraced his bride.

'Edward!' she called. 'I have wished for so very long,
For you to come here, take me, and sing me our song,'
They hurried to the door, trying to run away,
But the groom knew how to make sure Edward would stay.

He drew his trusty gun from the band at his hip,
The bride took the bullet, 'I love you,' on her lip,
The look of utter dismay was matched by both men,
The groom cried out, 'Well it is time for a duel then!'

Edward said, 'No, because for the rest of my life,
I will always be mourning this terrible strife,
I searched for five years for this damsel in distress,
I hope you think of her, dead in her wedding dress.'

**Kate McLaughlin (13)**
**Wallington High School for Girls, Wallington**

## The Ballad Of The Broken Curse

'Twas a long time ago where an island stood
Filled with darkness upon the gusty trees and wood,
Amongst all the branches a tower lay
With mouldy, cobbled walls that were always grey.

In this tower, there was a young girl named Lynn
Who had blonde, wavy hair and fair pale skin.
Her lips like rubies, her cheeks like the dawn of day
Her dark blue eyes glittering in the sun's ray.

All day she would sit in the tower alone,
No friends, no family, no love she had none.
For there was a wicked curse cast above
She could only escape when she found true love.

Her life was not worth living, there was no fun,
She wanted to kill herself so searched for a gun.
Lynn lifted it up and placed it by her head,
With one big blow and a bang she could soon be dead.

Suddenly he boldly kicked down the locked door
Poor Lynn was surprised at what she then saw,
He said so proudly, 'I am Tom, the baker's son,'
And with one big thrust he knocked away the gun.

His hair was a dark brown, and he was very thin,
A bunch of lace sat under his pale chin,
His trousers like night, his black boots up to the thigh,
His dark brown eyes glittering in the jewelled sky.

'Twas like a moth to a flame, Lynn fell in love
At last the curse was broken, so flew a white dove.
They had their first lover's kiss, and romantic song,
So here we have it, the pretty Lynn, and the handsome Tom.

**Laura Blake (13)**
**Wallington High School for Girls, Wallington**

**181**

# The Ballad Of True Love

Sophie was a girl adored by everyone,
Her hair was as bright as our Earth's natural sun.
Her dad was rich; she had a spoilt life,
Every man around wanted her as a wife.

Ben lived in a cottage with his old mum,
He was as poor as a church mouse, not rich like some.
He worked with the horses each long day,
Shovelling and rubbing for almost no pay.

Sophie's dad was known to all as Lord Frank,
Sophie was in awe, in fact from him she shrank.
He was a man used to his own way,
And he'd already planned Sophie's wedding day.

Sophie loved horses and oft went to ride,
Ben would hold her horse and help her get astride.
So then they would talk for hours on end,
Sophie realised she loved him more than a friend.

Then one summer morning, Lord Frank declared,
He had a wedding day for Sophie prepared.
'Twas to man who worked in the city,
He wanted a wife and thought Sophie pretty.

What a disaster, she could not bear it,
So she ran to find Ben, this news to share it.
'My love!' he cried, 'Marry me instead,'
'Ben, my father won't let me to you be wed.'

The two young lovers then plotted and planned
They knew for their future they must take a stand
One moonlit night two figures were seen
Escaping together off into their dream.

**Ashleigh Sullivan (13)**
**Wallington High School for Girls, Wallington**

## The Ballad Of The Last Love

Many nights together they spent,
In each other's arms Joe Leant,
And told Rosie, 'Our love is real,'
But something he must reveal.

Placed in the woods amongst the trees,
Rosie's hair flow'd in the breeze,
Underneath the stars shining bright,
Her soft skin so pale and white.

'I must leave, I can't be with you,'
His voice so sincere but blue,
He left her sitting on her own,
For her to cry, weep and moan.

Many years later she moved on,
As bright as the sun she shone,
In her beautiful, long, white robe,
Marrying her new love, Sir Cobe.

United together they were,
But something was miss'd in her,
On his tod, Joe miss'd her with love,
Cursing at the sky above.

'I must go back,' Joe said alone,
And found her not on her own,
'Who is this impostor?' Joe asked,
'He's the love I found at last.'

Then came a short moment of hush,
Leaving Rosie not to flush,
'Neither of you are the man for me,'
She then lived on merrily!

**Claire Harper (13)**
**Wallington High School for Girls, Wallington**

**183**

# The Ballad Of The Naïve

So beautiful she was,
She filled all others with love,
To look at her could make you cry,
So beautiful she was.

So hard to please she was
All of this was because,
She met a man that took her heart,
So hard to please she was.

So very loved she was,
That's a fact not known of,
She'd make all men stop and stare,
So very loved she was.

So ignorant she was,
As she knew not of this love,
This man loved her more than his own life,
So ignorant she was.

So unknowing she was,
She had a best friend Ross,
She did not know he loved her so,
So unknowing she was.

So very shocked she was,
When she heard her friend, Ross,
Say how he felt about his friend,
So very shocked she was.

So very hurt she was,
At the sound of this secret,
Ross would die - he was ill,
So very hurt she was.

**Toni Ibironke (13)**
**Wallington High School for Girls, Wallington**

184

## The Ballad Of Boston The Two Timer!

There once was young Boston, who was pale as a slave,
But he grew up to be beefed and at least he shaved,
And all the young ladies in the fair town would say,
'Will I ever be with Boston by the end of May?'

For there he stood and stared like a sheep wasting life,
Dreaming and drooling about the princess to be his wife,
He said to himself, 'But I am in love with another lady,'
He wasn't sure to propose to both as one of them was crazy.

*Bang! Crash! Wallop!* I will propose to both,
Whoever turns up to the wedding will be my fair oath,
But if they both turn up I will like toast,
I could imagine the scene, I'll be burned to roast.

'My dear Princess will you marry me?' he asked,
For she went red and stared with her cherry glass,
'I shall! I shall!' she said with enthusiasm and rhythm,
For now I have made my final decision.

I will ask Anastasia, 'Will you marry me?'
She also went red like a tomato cherry,
'Of course, of course,' she said like an energetic runner bean,
I will do anything to be with thee.

For now I have asked my ladies to marry,
No longer will I have to be on my Larry,
For now the day has come no one had turned up,
Wait, I hear a bang for I can't see anyone close-up.

*Bang! Bang!* Out of the blue are two brides with guns too,
For they have shot young Boston, upset and had no clue,
That what he did, he belonged in the wild zoo,
As Boston lies there dead and young out of the blue.

**Roshni Patel (12)**
**Wallington High School for Girls, Wallington**

**185**

# The Ballad Of Sir Gordon And Lissa

Sir Gordon and Lissa lived two separate lives,
They were happy but didn't feel complete inside.
Then one night they met just out of town,
And they knew they belonged at each other's side.

For many months they were happier than ever,
Then he decided with her he wanted to be.
So one night on his knee he did bend,
And she said yes with a smile full of glee.

So then they got married and lived by the harbour,
But there was one small problem, no money had he.
Every day the landlord came knocking,
And every day he did leave without his fee.

Until one morning he had had enough,
'Pay me now or you will be packing all your stuff.'
And so Lissa felt she had no choice,
She grabbed a knife and stabbed him with all her puff.

The very next day there was a knock on the door,
With her hands shaking she tried to stay tough.
But Sir Gordon swiftly stepped in front,
And instead it was him stuck in the handcuffs.

Then soon he was beheaded for what she had done,
She knew it should have been her on the chopping block.
So she walked down to the water's edge,
And was soon found floating on the shipping dock.

Sir Gordon and Lissa lived two separate lives,
They were happy but didn't feel complete inside.
Then one night they met just out of town,
And they knew they belonged at each other's side.

**Sarah Everett (13)**
**Wallington High School for Girls, Wallington**

## The Ballad Of The Chain Link Fence

The chain link fence across the block,
It helped the bad they said.
The bad would go, and come out good,
Exclaimed the sign I read.

But not all souls abandoned there,
Were there for doing wrong.
Like young Jesse boy, good as gold,
With heart and mind so strong.

A terrible life he did have,
No mum, no life, no dad.
The tragic blaze took more than wealth,
His family, so sad.

Not a happy lad oh was he,
He thought there was no love.
Until he met fair Mary-Lou,
His mind was free like doves.

So happy in love with Mary,
It seemed there was no end.
His heart again was a-beaming,
She was a true love send.

But one dark morning Jesse called,
Out to his love so dear.
No answer followed, what was wrong?
He cried a single tear.

Jesse was taken to the cell,
Charged for his poor wife's death.
But how he sighed as no one knew,
He did not take her breath.

**Lydia Hunter (13)**
**Wallington High School for Girls, Wallington**

# The Ballad Of Tragic Lovers

In a faraway place there was a girl,
Her name was Loopy and she was as bright as a pearl.
She had a father, who wished for her to marry,
A fair, rich man was he, with name as Garry.

She had no love for this stranger Garry,
As at heart she loves the sweet, innocent guy, Barry.
She had tried so hard to endorse her father to let her go with Barry,
But her father still wished for her to marry Garry.

Loopy sat whilst tears rolled down her face;
She looked in the mirror and thought, *what a disgrace.*
As she walked down the aisle she thought of her true love,
She turned her head and saw Barry; and flew to him like a dove.

They jumped on a horse and rode as fast as they could,
She didn't dare to look back; as if she would.
When they were far, far away they leaped off the horse,
And landed on the floor with such a great force.

Loopy grabbed Barry and lovingly remarked,
'I truly endeavour to love thee with all my heart.
And never do I imagine us to be apart,
In this lifetime or the next, nothing will stop me from loving you.'

But before they knew it a massive big cart,
Came riding, riding only to tear them apart.
Garry bounced out only to get out his sharp sword,
And sliced Barry to pieces, he stood up, expecting an award.

He grabbed Loppy and forced her to marry;
She was never happy and would always think of Barry.
And one day she had enough, so she picked up a sword,
And killed herself as she prayed to her Lord.

**Lisa Sivakumar (13)**
**Wallington High School for Girls, Wallington**

**188**

## The Ballad Of Hearts Entwined

There once was a charming young man,
And through his mind that young girl ran,
She was as fair as a dove,
Coming from heavens above.

He was just a poor stable boy,
But was happy and full of joy,
Jasper's heart and soul were pure,
Could she love him? He wasn't sure.

But young Jasper wouldn't let go,
He would go to her and then show,
His dear love and devotion,
There's no mistake or confusion.

With no more thought he took a horse,
He knew that this might take some force,
But he was willing to try,
And on his heart he would rely.

He saw her and came to a stop,
Cried, 'April, I love you a lot . . .
Whenever I think of you,
All I want is to be with you.'

April looked up curiously,
'Stable-boy . . .'she breathed cautiously,
'Jasper . . . I've looked, and found you,
This feeling is so true.'

He swung her up onto the horse,
And didn't feel any remorse,
They rode away together,
It didn't matter, he loved her.

**Lilla Porkolab (13)**
**Wallington High School for Girls, Wallington**

# The Ballad Of The Broken Dream

Here is a story of a young dame,
She was tall and pale, Scarlett was her name,
So happy and caring was she now,
About to marry and give her vow.

With dark blue eyes and long brunette hair,
She and Anthony would make a pair,
He was her hero, he was her knight,
Rode on horseback and shone in the light.

Until one day, a man rang the bell,
Grabbed her arm and led her to a cell,
He said he wanted her as his wife,
It seemed like she would stay there for life.

She screamed and cried but no one to help,
'Someone save me,' she started to yelp,
She soon gave up and lost all her hope,
She began weeping and couldn't cope.

At last she heard a gallop outside,
Anthony came running by her side,
Suddenly he fell onto the floor,
Soon he was lying, covered in gore.

Poor Anthony was struck by a sword,
He'd gone forever, she was assured,
She could not believe what she just saw,
Everything had gone wrong, just like a war.

She got hold of the sword, raised it high,
Said to herself, 'I might as well die,'
Moments later everything was calm,
And that was the end of their sweet charm.

**Sona Shah (13)**
**Wallington High School for Girls, Wallington**

## The Ballad Of Romeo And Juliet: An Alternative Ending

She was dressed into long and white,
Her fair hair tied up into a bow.
The dark eyes against her pale skin,
And so she waited all through the night.

He came to her in black and cream,
His silhouette outlined in the sun,
A face that had been carved by angels,
Stood tall before her like in a dream.

She was beautiful, so was he,
Under the orchard of blossomed buds,
He bent over onto the ground,
'Juliet, will you marry me?'

With no doubt in her singing voice,
She spoke without no hesitation,
'My Romeo, my heart is yours;
You are the only one, my choice'

The sun rose like a sparkling jewel;
And so dawned the day of the marriage,
The trusted gathered in the church,
The bride came riding on a mule

So then to clasp her lover's hand,
She slipped on a ring and she was his,
They turned to face the cheering crowd,
He swung her up into his arms, and

Kissed her, then ran through the tall arch,
They had been announced bride and groom,
They kissed again, then through the door,
Running into the open, blue spring dark.

**Ella Ifill-Williams (12)**
**Wallington High School for Girls, Wallington**

# The Ballad Of Runaway Love

There was a young seamstress who dreamt for some work;
She was beautiful so men would often lurk.
One day she took a ride to the prince's land,
She rode all day leaving prints in the sand.

Prince Eric was sitting calmly on his throne;
He felt a strong presence, he was not alone.
His liquid eyes lifted and what did he see?
A raggedy seamstress, 'She's the one for me.'

It was love at first sight for both of them so;
Their eyes connected, chemistry was not low.
Sparks were flying, the air was extremely hot.
Their eyes parted, they could be together not.

A great shame for they could not be seen a pair,
But they knew forever the love they would share.
The light room was empty from what he could see,
*Please just one kiss,* he said in a mental plea.

An idea popped into Prince Eric's head;
It was risky and if found out they would be dead.
The idea was to meet undercover,
Without being discovered by his mother.

In secret they met when the night was still dark;
They embraced one another in the dim park.
One day they stayed out there all day and all night,
But they were not expecting such a big fright.

The mother came strolling into the dim light;
She was angry and drew her sword for a fight.
The prince grabbed the girl, together they would run,
Far into the distance of the setting sun.

**Elizabeth Basusi (12)**
**Wallington High School for Girls, Wallington**

**192**

## The Ballad Of Love At Last

Over the bridge and the gleaming lake,
Across the fields of green;
Under the willows, on a country road,
A cottage can be seen.

And further down the beautiful road,
A girl walked down the street;
No one who loved her and no one to love,
She searched for someone sweet.

And then she saw him, her one true love,
Upon a fallen tree;
And when he saw her he stopped and he stared,
She approached him quietly.

'Please, Sir,' she whispered desperately,
'I have nowhere to stay,
I'm praying for a roof above my head,
I've wandered through the day.'

The boy looked at this desperate girl,
So lonely, lost and sad;
'Come my love, and stay with me if you wish,'
He smiled to see her glad.

They crossed the bridge and the gleaming lake,
Across the fields they went;
They went underneath the old willow trees,
In that cottage she dreamt.

For many years they lived together,
So deep in love were they,
And so we come to the end of this tale,
That I have told today.

**Beth Gates (13)**
**Wallington High School for Girls, Wallington**

193

# The Ballad Of Two Worlds Apart

Two worlds apart were Justin and Briee,
For her he was a star out of the sky;
For him she was everything my, oh my.
Two worlds apart were these lovers.

They met one day at a meet and greet,
As she walked over he jumped out of his seat.
He said, 'You must wait till after, we need to speak?'
Two worlds apart were these lovers.

Her beautiful brown hair blew gently in the wind,
Her fringe covered her sparkly eyes within;
Her rosy red lips moved as she started to sing.
Two worlds apart were these lovers.

His hair was a shiny brown too.
The paper he was signing went a flew,
So he let it fly and got a new.
Two worlds apart were these lovers.

The paper landed at Briee's feet,
She looked at it and cried in deceit.
With teary eyes she waited to meet.
Two worlds apart were these lovers.

A love letter was on the stone.
He came and explained the words he has sewn.
She smiled and said, 'I should have known.'
Two worlds apart were these lovers.

He flicked his hair to one side,
And looked into her dreamy eyes;
As they shared a passionate lover's kiss
Two hearts as one were these lovers.

**Mehru Raza (13)**
**Wallington High School for Girls, Wallington**

## The Ballad Of The Fake Love

The birds were flying in the air; their wings were flapping,
There was a vast crowd standing on the grass clapping,
Every one were acclaiming and were so ecstatic,
There were two lovers and they were in an attic.

Surrounding the small attic were the people cheering,
There stood the lovers' friends and family hearing,
The girl was called Carry and she wanted to marry,
The boy loved Carry so much and was called Barry.

Carry was so pulchritudinous and alluring,
She was enthusiastic and was not boring,
Her beautiful cheeks were red as a smashing rose,
She was very cute so every boy liked the pose.

On a luminous day Barry went to the village,
He saw a rich girl standing on a bridge,
Barry was very shocked so he went to talk to her,
He said, 'You are cute and your hair is like a fur!'

He asked, 'Please madam, can you tell me what your name is?'
She was called pretty Paige; they were going to kiss,
Because they loved each other so much they got carried,
Paige was rich; Barry's horrible heart was carried.

While Barry was having fun with Paige, Carry was sad,
She then realised that Barry was very bad,
She then went to his old village to see where he was,
Barry was lying with Paige with a bottle of glass.

'I loved you so much but you never loved me!' she said,
He said, 'I hate you, so I will sleep on the bed.'
Barry was sad that she cried until all her tears ran out,
She died there with sorrow; with her fake love doubt.

**Nandhini Manoharan (12)**
**Wallington High School for Girls, Wallington**

# The Ballad Of Professor Pete's Love

The wedding bells rang for young Billy and Lilly,
But lady Beth was so in love it was silly,
She loved young Bill as much as poor Pete loved her too,
Their words were so far apart but their love was so true.

Pete and Beth were so different in so many ways,
Beth was so rich she got one million a day,
But Pete was so poor he lived on his love for Beth,
Beth's love for silly Billy was driving Pete to death.

After the wedding was done, Beth got so depressed,
However her father could see she was a mess,
So he decided what he was going to do,
He needed a good jester but didn't know who.

He kept hiring and hiring, one, two, three,
But then walked in Sir Pete, was he the one to be?
He said a few jokes, she laughed and they fell in love,
Pete told Beth, 'You are a gift from above.'

They went to a banquet and shared their first dance,
He stole a kiss from her cheek, their love was enhanced,
The couple went to a park and they had a picnic,
Pete was running out of time, his clock went *tick-tock!*

'I love you my dear, our hearts together I need,'
Could this be marriage? It's what she hoped it to be,
Sir Pete told Lady Beth, 'You are the one for me,'
Then he pulled out a ring and got down on one knee.

'Will you be mine, will you be mine?'
'Yes.' said she,
They will be together for eternity.

**Rachael Butcher (13)**
**Wallington High School for Girls, Wallington**

## The Ballad Of The Only Woman For Me

Her name was Heather,
We used to be together.
But now we're apart,
She broke my beating heart.
I'm under the weather,
I'm like a little feather,
Just by myself.

She was so beautiful,
She was so wonderful.
Her golden hair was so fair,
Her nose was like a rose.
Especially when she did a pose,
Her lips were sweet, she never lied.

She was so sweet,
You would want to weep.
Like blossoms in the spring,
You would want to sing.
Her smile was so sweet,
The birds would go *tweet, tweet,*
She made my heart want to fly.

She was for me,
I was for her.
She looked at me with her gentle eyes,
And I knew this was my final goodbye.
I kissed her lips and cried a tear,
And said, 'Oh my sweet dear,'
And my beating heart became very still.

**Majurapathy Nimalan (13)**
**Wallington High School for Girls, Wallington**

197

# The Ballad Of Helena And The Dreamer

Helena and Samson were to be wed,
She was a true beauty with cheeks of red,
He had lime-green eyes and dreamed of above,
He was a raven, yet she was a dove;
Could've lasted forever, but that's love.

Helena and Samson were out in town,
Then jewels from the sky came tumbling down;
Samson the dreamer looked up to the moon,
Then he said, 'Come my dear, we will fly soon,'
Their song was of love but soon changed its tune.

Helena and Samson were off to fly,
After they'd wed they announced their goodbye,
They were off to where no one liv'd before,
They were to break all rules, defy the law;
So naive of heartbreak that lay before.

Helena and Samson were taking off,
'Hoer,' the engine let out a big cough;
Helena announced, 'I can't!' with appeal,
Then Samson removed his hands from the wheel,
With more emotion than a man could feel.

Helena and Samson went sep'rate ways;
Ev'ry full moon Helena's in a daze,
She thinks of the dreamer that lives afar,
And how he left her for that twinkling star,
The woe of Helena and the dreamer.

**Toni Ayonrinde (13)**
**Wallington High School for Girls, Wallington**

198

## Chowder

Chowder oh chowder, like baking powder with a bellow
Shrieking sound that gets louder and louder.

The bellowing sound of thy chowder is like being locked
Away in a tower with no shower.

Thy chowder, thy chowder, the way you eat must be
A heck of a beat.

The way you eat a bunch of food you really munch until
You barf down the loo.

The way you're escaping from the beast, at least be nice
Before you feast.

If it's food that you want, find it, heat it, eat it before it's
Taken by the foodnapper.

Run, run, before you're kissed and called bun-bun by
Panini.

**Hugh Penrhyn-Lowe (12)**
**West Hill School, Leatherhead**

## Love Poem

She saw me
Then she kissed me
On the cheek.

She loved me
For ever and ever.

She gave me her number
We went to the park
The shops
And then a barbeque.

Then I took her home
And the next day
I went back to live my dream again.

**Connor Beattie (12)**
**West Hill School, Leatherhead**

**199**

## Crystal Palace

C rowd were going mad, Crystal Palace won the Coca Cola
   championship
R esult
Y ou could hear a pin drop when Crystal Palace scored a goal 20
   yards out
S ide tackle
T icking the clock
A ll eyes on the pitch
L ove of the game

P alace players playing their hearts out
A ll to play for
L ove of the club
A mbrose scores an amazing goal
C hampions
E nd of season, bring on next season.

**Ciaran Marren (12)**
**West Hill School, Leatherhead**

## Age Of The Reptiles

The lifetime of giants and dwarfs
Youth and knowledge are your strengths
You are the lords of the elements
Rulers of the skies, the lands and waters
Rulers of the ice, the deserts and the forest
They were terrible, peaceful and modest
Kings and queens
They were the rulers of time
The mystic rulers of space
They were the greatest creatures on Earth
And we remember them as the
Dinosaurs.

**Alex Freeman (14)**
**West Hill School, Leatherhead**

## My Best Friend

Dogs like to bury bones.
They eat my shoes sometimes.
Dogs jump up, ganging up together.
They lie in the sun.
They go in the shade.
They leave, going to the park and fetching the bone.
They bark when they are hungry.
They bark when they see another dog.
They bark when they want to protect.
Sometimes they bark just for fun.

**Courtney Murphy (12)**
**West Hill School, Leatherhead**


## A Magical Thing

Weather, weather, weather,
My dad, Trevor, said that the weather is such a magical thing.
He's always said that the lightning crashes and the sun smiles and
that's why we have sunshine.
But the moon you see is not the nicest thing,
That's why no one goes out at night.
My dad, Trevor, said that the rain comes from the sky,
But everyone knows that,
So the weather, weather, weather is such a magical thing.

**Chelsea Cooke (13)**
**West Hill School, Leatherhead**


## My Dog Rupert

R upert is my pride and joy
U sually he sits on me
P oo is what I call him
E verywhere I am he is there
R upert is my best friend
T ogether we go everywhere.

**Cory Andrews (11)**
**West Hill School, Leatherhead**

## Autumn

A utumn is golden
U nder the sunset it is like the sky is on fire
T he bees pollinate in summer
U p in the sky it's so pitch-black
M ist looks like the grass is on fire
N ight sky looks like ash.

**Jason Jackson (12)**
**West Hill School, Leatherhead**

## Autumn

A utumn
U nder the trees are leaves
T rees are losing leaves
U nder the cold trees are brown leaves
M ud is on your shoes
N ewts are under the logs.

**Ricky Allen (11)**
**West Hill School, Leatherhead**

## Mice

I love mice because they are nice
Even though they don't like rice.
Sometimes when I check on my mouse
It always escapes in the house.
Still I love mice because they are still nice.

**Amy Armstrong (11)**
**West Hill School, Leatherhead**

## Tonight I Went And Took A Ride On My Bike

Beautiful, romantic, not strong enough
Words for what it is really like.
Nothing on the road but me and my metal.
The soft, chilled winds flow through the pedals.
The street lights are like candles, they light
Up the floor.
All the surroundings, it's hard to keep going
With such things to adore.
The pace is quick but as not to miss the face details.
You cannot analyse the lovely side of monster
Cars and noisy rails.
Everything around, now just feels so pretty.
Feeling my road beneath my ride, it's soft,
It's eerie, although, yet, gritty.
Long or short it's just one simple pleasure.
It's a lovely getaway from what of life is a pester.

**Peter Tampin-Copp (15)**
**Wey Valley School, Dorset**

# Young Writers Information

We hope you have enjoyed reading this book - and that you will continue to enjoy it in the coming years.

If you like reading and writing poetry drop us a line, or give us a call, and we'll send you a free information pack.

Alternatively if you would like to order further copies of this book or any of our other titles, then please give us a call or log onto our website at www.youngwriters.co.uk.

Young Writers Information
Remus House
Coltsfoot Drive
Peterborough
PE2 9JX
(01733) 890066